Wanted In Rome

Living and loving in the Eternal City

Maggie Johnston

PEACOCK
Publications

Published by Peacock Publications
38 Sydenham Road, Norwood, South Australia
Copyright © Margaret Johnston
First published June, 2009
National Library of Australia Card Number & ISBN 1 921601 35 4
Printed by Peacock Publications, Adelaide

In the heart of every man, wherever he is born, whatever his education and tastes there is one small corner which is Italian, that part which finds regimentation irksome, the dangers of war frightening, strict morality stifling, that part which loves frivolous and entertaining art, admires larger than life size solitary heroes, and dreams of an impossible liberation from the strictures of a tidy existence.

Dott. Luigi Barzini
The Italians

To Mensie,

Hope you enjoy it!

Love Margaret.

June 2009,

For my beautiful granddaughters:
Olivia, Kaylee and Georgina.

Author's Note

The following memoir is based on facts taken from diary notes and my recollections.

In certain instances I have changed the names of people involved. I have not been able to recall actual conversations verbatim, and have therefore needed to reconstruct dialogue. What I have written is consistent with the facts available to me, and my memory. The sequence of events may not be entirely correct; however, to the best of my knowledge and ability, it is an accurate account of my two years in Rome.

Maggie Johnston

Contents

Prelude	11
All Roads Lead to Rome	13
Bella Roma	29
The English Teacher	44
Piazza Navona	50
The Fountains of Rome	57
Natale	62
Villa Borghese	64
Amici	71
Cats and Dogs	85
Oscar Night	88
Halcyon Days	95
The Baptism	100
Troppo Caldo!	105
Innamorata	111
Soul Mates	117
A New Apartment	125

Latin Lover 134

Death's Door. 136

Guardia Di Finanza 144

Daylight Robbery 151

The Churches of Rome 157

Looking for Shoes 162

The Love Bunnies 165

The Eternal City 168

Arrivederci Roma 173

Epilogue 181

Acknowledgements 183

Prelude

The Boeing 737 rises majestically into the late summer sky, banks around and points its nose south-east. I close my eyes and grip the armrests. I'm a member of the 'white knuckle brigade'. Flying is not my favourite mode of transport.

Within minutes we reach a cruising altitude of thirty-five thousand feet. I feel the plane level off and the noise of the engines change from a laboured screech to a gentle drone. I exhale and open my eyes. Below us, the fluffy white nimbus clouds appear like a carpet of candy floss, tinted pink in the morning sun.

Earlier, the taxi taking me to Heathrow Airport had needed to make a detour over Chelsea Bridge, so we arrived at the airport late. The line at the check-in counter was a mile long and was moving painfully slow. Eventually, I was facing the desk clerk.

'I'd like a seat as far forward as possible please. On the jump seat in the cockpit or on the pilot's lap would be preferable.'

Because of my fear of flying I made the same request every time I flew. Usually my request raises a laugh, although I am deadly serious. I reckon if the plane's going to ditch, I'm better off with the pilot!

Once upon a time I had wanted to be an air hostess, as they were called in those days, and had applied for a position with a major airline. I was interviewed by a panel of company bigwigs, which was pretty nerve-wracking. A week later I received a 'regret' letter, stating that I did not meet the criteria because I was underweight, but that if I were to gain a few pounds I could reapply.

Now, looking at the stewardesses—some fat, some thin, some short, some tall, and all ages—I wonder at what stage that criteria had ceased to become important.

Why I had ever wanted that career, considering my fear of flying, was a puzzle to both my friends and myself. But now even fear cannot dampen my excitement. I am pursuing a dream of living and working in Italy. My destination: The Eternal City, Rome.

I recline the seat, close my eyes, and let my mind wander back to the first trip I made to Italy, almost twenty years ago. . .

All Roads Lead to Rome

All roads, howso'er they diverge
Lead to Rome
BOREY

I'd had a love affair with Italy since I was a teenager. When all my friends were jetting off to the Costa del Sol in Spain, I was drooling over holiday brochures of Italy. It wasn't until several years later, in the mid-seventies, that I finally visited the land of my dreams.

Having finished a four-year contract as a private secretary to the Managing Director of a prestigious London hotel, I needed a break. I decided this was my opportunity to take off to Italy.

I started my holiday in Florence, with the intention of travelling around Tuscany and then on to Rome. I can still remember the train steaming into Santa Maria Nouvella Station, and the blue sign on the platform with large white letters that announced FIRENZE.

Florence! The very name conjures up art, architecture, David, Dante, Il Duomo; the home of noble Florentine families such as the Medici and Pitti.

I fell in love with the place, with the people, and with one man in particular. Marco was fair skinned, with light brown curly hair and a moustache. I'm not usually attracted to men with moustaches, but, with his twinkling blue eyes and dazzling white smile, it gave him a rather attractive, rakish air.

He approached me while I was taking photographs in the Piazza della Signoria, and offered to take my photograph beside Michelangelo's statue of David—a replica, the original is in the

Accademia—which stands outside the Palazzo Vecchio. I had noticed him earlier standing by the Neptune fountain, dressed casually, but smartly, in a pale pink shirt and blue jeans.

'*Piacere, mi chiamo Marco,*' he offered his hand.

'*Io sono Margaret,*' I replied.

I liked the way his hand felt in mine, warm and firm.

'Would you like to drink coffee?' he asked, in English.

He *was* rather dishy.

'Yes, I'd love to,' I answered casually.

We sat at one of the little bars that surround the piazza and talked. He spoke very good English.

'How long are you in Florence?'

'I'm just passing through on my way to Rome,' I answered.

He looked surprised. 'You cannot come to Firenze for only one day. There is too much to see. You are very welcome to stay in my apartment.'

I had come to Italy for a cultural holiday, but of course I was secretly hoping for a romantic encounter. This could be it. I definitely would like to see more of this man, but should I agree to stay with him having only known him an hour? What would he think of me? More to the point, what would my friends think if they knew that within a few hours of arriving in Italy I'm shacked up with someone? My mind was in turmoil. Then I remembered my friend Fran's words to me before I left London. 'You only regret the things you don't do.'

'I'd love to, but I could book into a hotel,' I ventured.

'Please,' he insisted. 'You stay at my apartment, I stay with my mother.'

It was too good an opportunity to miss.

'Fine,' I relented, 'but just for tonight.' What harm could I come to?

He paid for the coffees and, taking me by the arm, led me down a side street off the piazza to where his car, a little red Fiat, was parked. We drove through the streets of Florence until we reached a *palazzo* not far from the centre. Explaining that it was his mother's house, he jumped out of the car. '*Aspetta!* I will be one moment.' He disappeared into the building. About fifteen minutes later, he reappeared with his arms full of linens and towels and placed them in the boot of the car.

We drove back towards the centre and stopped in a narrow street where Marco skilfully manoeuvred his car into a tight space, leaving it half on the pavement and half on the road. From the street we stepped through a large wooden door that opened onto a *cortile*—an open internal courtyard—with apartment buildings on three sides. Winding up the exterior of the building opposite was a spiral staircase. At the top of the staircase a door led into his apartment which was small, but appeared clean and well furnished. It consisted of an open-plan kitchen, dining and lounge area, bathroom and, at the rear of the apartment, a raised platform on which stood a large antique bed. Marco busied himself stripping the bed and remaking it. He showed me the bathroom and put out some clean towels.

'Fai come se fossi a casa tua,' he smiled. I guessed this was the equivalent of 'make yourself at home'.

'I come take you to dinner at eight o'clock.' Then as he turned to go he added, 'Oh please, not to open the refrigerator.' And with that he was gone!

I threw myself on the freshly made bed. Who would believe it, here I am in Florence—no Firenze sounds so much better—in a lovely apartment, and about to go to dinner with a dishy Italian man.

I danced into the bathroom, showered as best I could in the drizzle of water that escaped from the showerhead, and deliberated on what to wear. Marco hadn't given me any indication as to the type of restaurant he was taking me to, formal or casual. I opted for a happy medium and chose a mid-length red skirt with a halter-neck top, and a pair of black sandals with a wedge heel. I checked my reflection in the mirror. I've always wished that my nose was smaller and my lips fuller, but my eyes are large and green and my crowning glory is my red hair.

I was ready early, and had a few minutes to wait for Marco. Suddenly I felt very vulnerable. What was I thinking of? I didn't know this man from Adam! What if he didn't come? What if he *did* come?

He came, and swept me off my feet!

Marco was very romantic and generous, with a good sense of humour. We got on famously, so when he asked me to stay on in Florence with him, I didn't hesitate. I stayed in Florence for three months and never made it to Rome!

Marco had moved back into his apartment within a few days of my arrival, by which time, of course, I had opened the forbidden refrigerator. My curiosity had got the better of me. What if he was really a serial killer and there were chopped up body parts in the fridge, or a drug dealer with a fridge full of narcotics? Maybe even a gun. *I had to open the fridge!*

Gingerly, I opened the door a crack, standing well back, and peeked inside from a distance. Shock, horror! A swarm of tiny flies escaped, as an odour like sulphur hit my nostrils. I closed the door quickly, but not before I had seen the contents. There were no body parts, no drugs, no gun, just lots of empty broken eggshells. This man obviously loved omelettes! But why was he preserving the shells? Maybe it was some peculiar Italian custom? No, I thought to myself. He's just too lazy to take them out to the rubbish bin.

I never revealed to Marco that I'd opened the refrigerator. One day I arrived back at the apartment from one of my art gallery trips to find him cooking in the kitchen, using provisions from the freshly cleaned fridge.

Marco's father was a shirtmaker who owned a factory near Florence. According to tradition, Marco was expected to carry on the family business, although he had absolutely no interest in it. His apathy was tolerated because he was the owner's son. He managed one of his father's shops in the centre of Florence and sometimes I called in to see him. I loved to run my hands over the shiny walnut counter, which felt smooth and warm to the touch. The matching walnut shelves that lined the walls were stacked with neatly folded cotton shirts in every colour imaginable, from white through the whole colour spectrum to black.

Occasionally, Marco and I would leave the apartment together in the mornings. Marco would greet people in the street with: *'Ciao, dov'e vai?'* to which would come the response, *'Lavoro.'*

It was only after I'd been there a few weeks that I learned these people were going to work, and not to the launderette to do their washing. Although in general my Italian was improving, I had confused the verb *lavorare*, to work, with *lavare*, to wash.

Most days when Marco worked, I would go to the Uffizi Gallery, Florence's famous art gallery. I hardly glanced at the beautiful sculptures and works of art that lined the corridors, beneath exotically painted ceilings. The thought of the Sandro Botticelli masterpieces propelled me along the marble tiled floor straight to the Sala del Botticelli. I would sit for long stretches of time gazing in rapture at *The Birth of Venus*, which depicts the lovely Venus, with long titian-coloured hair and white skin, rising from a seashell. She is draped in a diaphanous gown. A nymph stands beside her. Looking on is the wind god, Zephyrus—the west wind, bringer of light spring and early-summer breezes—who is holding the nymph Chloris.

My other favourite Botticelli painting, *La Primavera*—spring—depicts Mercury the winged messenger, the Three Graces, Venus, Zephyrus the wind god, and the nymph Chloris. Above the figures, Cupid points his arrow towards Venus. I love the style of Botticelli's elongated female forms.

Other days I walked over the Ponte Vecchio, the oldest bridge in Florence, which spans the River Arno. The bridge is lined with exquisite jewellers' shops and I would spend some time gazing in the windows before continuing on to the spectacular renaissance Giardino di Boboli, next to the Pitti Palace. I loved the quietness of this garden. For me it was a lush green oasis away from the hustle and bustle of the city.

Often I would walk down the Viottolone, a white-pebbled avenue of cypress trees, interspersed with classical marble statues. The avenue sweeps down to a small artificial lake, *Isolotto*, around which a few stone benches are placed. I found it a peaceful spot to sit and read, in the shade of the rich green cypress trees encircling the lake.

My favourite statue in the gardens was the impressive white-marble sculpture of Pegasus, the winged horse, rearing up on hind legs, wings spread, ready to bear him up to the Tuscan sky. I read in my guidebook that Pegasus figures in the Greek myth of the hero Bellerophon. According to the myth, Bellerophon slew the Chimera, a monstrous creature with a lion's head, a goat's body and a dragon's tail, and then attempted to fly Pegasus all the way to heaven, but fell off. Pegasus kept on flying, ultimately taking his home in the stars as a constellation, which now bears his name.

On the way back to Marco's apartment I would invariably stop at Vivoli, a *gelateria* that I discovered on the Via dei Stinche, and choose an ice cream from the thirty-five different flavours. Occasionally, I sampled some of the flavours before making my choice, although I already knew it would be the delicious *pistacchio*!

Marco and I made love in the afternoons. Italians have an extended lunch break, so that they can have a *siesta* after eating and avoid the hottest part of the day. We usually arrived back at the apartment simultaneously just after noon and wasted no time on eating. He was an exciting lover and had the stamina of a horse—an Italian stallion! Often he wouldn't return to work, as we got so caught up in the moment, finally emerging from our cotton cocoon only to eat dinner.

Marco was well-known in Florence, and often we would meet up with his friends for dinner in the evenings. We usually went to small restaurants with no name, which were referred to as 'hole in the wall' eateries. The first time he took me for dinner to a hole in the wall, I thought we were visiting a friend's house.

One large table with several chairs around it stood in the centre of the room. A large Italian *mamma* appeared from the kitchen, her blue and white striped apron covered in flour. She greeted Marco affectionately, talking in rapid Italian and waving her arms animatedly, before retreating into her kitchen. (I had by now come to the conclusion that if Italians were to sit on their hands, they wouldn't be able to talk!) Within a few minutes she produced two large plates of spaghetti, which she proudly placed in front of us with a '*Buon appetito.*'

It was unlike any spaghetti I'd seen back home in England, where in most 'Italian' restaurants it would usually be smothered in some kind of tomato sauce. This was just plain unadorned spaghetti. I sprinkled it liberally with grated *parmigiano* cheese, hoping to give it some flavour. I tried to copy Marco and wind the slippery pasta around my fork without the help of a spoon. When the odd strand of spaghetti hung out of Marco's mouth, he just sucked it up and it disappeared into his mouth, like a long white worm.

At home I probably would have cut the pasta into shorter lengths, or bitten off the wayward strands hanging out of my mouth, letting them plop back onto my plate. When I eventually got some of the pasta into my mouth I had a delicious surprise. It tasted wonderful, although compared to the soft pasta I'd had back home it seemed slightly undercooked. Marco explained that pasta should be cooked *al dente*, which is just enough to be firm and not soft. This was my introduction to real Italian style spaghetti, and I loved it.

Some weekends Marco and I would ride up into the hills above Florence on his motorbike. We didn't wear crash helmets. The wind in my face and hair was exhilarating. En route we usually stopped at Piazzale Michelangelo to take in the panoramic views of Florence; Il Duomo di Santa Maria del Fiore visible in the distance, before continuing on to Fiesole, a little hilltop town, to eat lunch.

One weekend we drove to Pisa, where we acted like tourists, taking photographs of each other, arm outstretched, holding up the leaning tower!

After three months in Florence I realised I wasn't in love with Marco, but I was in love with Italy. I returned home, vowing that one day I would return to live there.

I dreamed of living in the Tuscan hills above Florence. Little did I know that an opportunity to do just that, would present itself to me sometime in the future.

* * *

I saw the writing on the wall, maybe twelve months before it happened.

I was a personal assistant to the director of a financial company based in London's West End.

Having been with the company for nearly ten years, I thought I would be there until I happily retired. I loved the work, and really looked forward to going into the office every morning. Every day was different. My boss, Michael, was middle-aged, tall and distinguished looking with a full head of silver-grey hair. He was a laid back kind of guy, and we worked well together.

'We have a good relationship don't we?' he used to say.

'Yes, a good *working* relationship,' I would jokingly retort.

Michael was happily married and I knew his wife quite well. If she was shopping in the city, she would call into the office and the three of us would have lunch together. Michael and Joan had two adult daughters, and I liked to think that they looked upon me as another daughter.

I had watched the company expand from its humble beginnings in a small historical-listed building near Marble Arch, to a whole floor of offices in prestigious Mayfair.

Michael had a brilliant idea to form a one-stop shop for financial services. His speciality was taxation advice, and he formed a partnership with an insurance advisor and a pension advisor, who moved into the new premises in Mayfair, along with their incumbent staff. His favourite saying was 'never get into a rut, because a rut is a shallow grave and a grave is a dead-end'.

In 1987 we were on a high. It was the Thatcher era. General elections had just been held and Maggie was now in her third term of office. Money flowed like water, and with it emerged the 'yuppies' with bottomless expense accounts and huge bonuses. Michael had a successful business and all the trimmings of a successful businessman: a town house in Mayfair, a country house in the stockbroker belt of Oxfordshire, a holiday apartment in the Canary Islands and his status symbol, a Rolls Royce. His success was rubbing off on us all. We were one big happy family of well-paid yuppies. They were the golden years of birthdays celebrated at the Ritz, or dinner at the famous Ivy and office parties at Café Royal for Christmas or New Year. There were numerous invitations to be wined and dined by wealthy overseas clients, who brought expensive gifts when they came to call. We were on a roll, living the high life.

One of the most memorable occasions was an invitation to an Indian wedding, the likes of which I'd never seen before. The son of a wealthy Indian client was to be married. The ceremony would be held in the renowned Great Room of the prestigious Grosvenor House Hotel on Park Lane. Over one thousand guests had been invited.

It was a riot of colour. The ladies in their saris looked like exotic butterflies. The groom arrived a few minutes ahead of the bride, dressed in white, from his turban to his shoes. He looked like a very handsome maharajah. His bride-to-be arrived in a long white limousine festooned with flowers, looking serenely beautiful in a red and gold sari.

Inside the Great Room, the bride and groom walked together on rose petals, strewn over a red carpet, to the flower-covered arbour where they took their marriage vows. They then made their way to a central stage where they sat, side by side, while their guests filed past them, shook their hands and handed them wedding gifts. A spectacular show followed with jugglers, Scottish pipers and a real live elephant, courtesy of Harrods. Stalls with cuisine from numerous countries were arranged around the room. What a lavish affair it was.

Finally, at three o'clock in the morning, the newlyweds left in a horse-drawn carriage and I was delivered home in style in Michael's Rolls Royce, feeling elated after such a wonderful cultural experience.

Looking back it's hard to pinpoint just when things started to go wrong with the company. With hindsight, Michael was overly ambitious and tried to expand too quickly, which left him with very little capital and many cash flow problems, ironic for a financial advisor. But we were doomed when certain shady characters started to call, proposing huge monetary gains from the sale and purchase of various commodities, a venture that needed a large sum of money to be paid up front from the buyer. Michael's role was to find a buyer and negotiate between the buyer and seller. They talked in millions of pounds and of escrow accounts. On a successful deal, as the agent, Michael would have a slice of the profits.

A huge amount of time and energy was spent trying to find buyers for these commodities, to the detriment of Michael's own clients, who were his 'bread and butter'. We lost some major clients, and so began the slippery slide. It became more and more difficult to find the cash to pay the bills and the employees' salaries. I was willing to forfeit some of my monthly salary in order to be able to pay the telephone bill. That was our lifeline. Without that we would be non-existent.

Michael never gave up hope that some big deal would materialise and we would all be rich. Of course, it never did come to fruition. He started to rely heavily on his other two partners for financial support, until eventually they dissolved the partnership and went their own way, leaving him with enormous unused office space for which he was paying a premium.

One by one my colleagues were let go, until only Michael and myself were left holding the fort. Creditors started to call asking for payment of outstanding invoices. 'The cheque's in the post' became my stock phrase.

Then one day the bailiffs turned up at the door. We managed to fob them off and had a short reprieve, until they showed up again six weeks later. Again we gave them promises that funds were expected and bills would be paid. They were empty promises.

The company struggled on for some months until finally we could not hold the wolves back from the door any longer. In the summer of 1993 we were forced to go into voluntary liquidation. I will never forget leaving the office and locking the doors behind us for the last time. It was the end of an era.

Before the demise of the company, I made a decision that would change the course of my life. Having just reached the big five-0, I was reluctant to find another PA position. I wanted to completely change direction. My daughter and my son were independent. I was a free spirit. So I decided to train to become an English teacher to foreign students, with the intention of working abroad.

I enrolled at Birkbeck College, London University, and just before the company went into liquidation I earned a TESOL—Teaching English to Speakers of Other Languages—certificate, my passport to many different countries.

Even though I'd been happy with my job, my mind had often wandered back to the rolling Tuscan hills and the wonderful, if brief, time I had spent there with Marco; so after considering offers to teach in far-flung countries like Japan or Vietnam, I decided on somewhere a little closer to home and to my heart, Italy!

* * *

Three encounters during the last twelve months of the company's trading eventually put me on the road to Rome.

Marie, a lifelong friend of mine who had moved to Los Angeles some years previously, introduced me to Gayle. They both worked in the film industry. Gayle had quit her job to fulfil an ambition to travel to Rome and, hopefully, find enough work to be able to support herself. She would be staying in London for two weeks en route and needed accommodation. Although I had never met Gayle, I invited her to stay with me.

I opened my door to a very attractive African American lady with a big wide smile. I liked her immediately and we got on like a house on fire. Gayle was very articulate and had an inimitable way of smiling as she talked. I practiced this myself in front of a mirror, without success.

During her stay with me, I mentioned to Gayle my situation at work and my love affair with Italy.

'So why not come with me honey?' she asked in her matter of fact way. She made everything seem so simple. 'Just do it.'

'I couldn't leave at the moment with the company in so much trouble, it would be like deserting a sinking ship,' I lamented.

'Well, let's keep in touch, and if you change your mind and want to come to Rome, just let me know.'

At the time I was also attending an evening school for Italian language lessons and became friendly with two of my fellow students, Patricia and Dawn. Patricia was some years older than me, a very knowledgeable and interesting lady, whose company I enjoyed. Dawn was several years younger than both of us, a very attractive, bubbly girl, with long hair that reached to her waist.

One evening, Dawn announced to the class that she was going to live in Rome. She had rented an apartment for six months, and although she did not have a job to go to, seemed pretty confident that she would find something. We were all very envious.

Before Dawn left England, she handed me her forwarding address. 'Don't forget to look me up if you ever decide to come to Rome.'

I was totally stressed out with everything that was happening with the company, which I knew was about to fold. I had to make some serious decisions and needed to get away for a while, so Patricia and I booked a language course at a school in Florence for two weeks. We would share an apartment in the centre within walking distance of the school.

Just before we left London I'd been idly leafing through *The Lady,* a magazine that advertises job vacancies abroad, mainly in the domestic field, and an advertisement caught my eye:

> Wanted—Mature responsible English lady for live-in governess position in Italy, Nr. Florence. 1 child, own room, car, good remuneration.
> Ref. I84526.

I telephoned the Agency. The vacancy was in Fiesole, in the hills above Florence. Explaining that I had a holiday booked in Florence later in the month, the Agency managed to set up an appointment for me to meet the advertiser, a lady called Flavia, to coincide with my trip to Florence.

Arriving in Florence brought on a sense of *déjà vu,* as memories of the three months spent with Marco came flooding back.

I wondered if Marco was still around. I considered trying

to find him, but almost twenty years had passed and I preferred to keep the three months that we'd spent together a happy memory.

On the appointed day of the interview, Patricia and I took the number 7 bus out of Florence up to the hilltop town of Fiesole.

It was quite an eventful ride. The bus was full, so we had to stand. A football match was being shown on television on the bus. Oh, how the Italians love their football!

The bus toiled up the steep winding road, leaving behind the heat and dust of Florence, and blocks of apartment buildings gave way to large private villas. After about ten minutes, Patricia looked at me with a strange expression on her face and said through gritted teeth:

'Let's move further down the bus.'

I looked at her as if she was mad—the bus was so crowded I could hardly move a muscle.

Then I felt a hand on my backside. Now I knew why she wanted to move. Not wanting to make a fuss, we didn't say a word to anyone, and did our best to move a little further along the bus out of reach of the groping hand. I thought that the days of pinching bottoms were gone, but obviously old habits die hard.

A few minutes later, an altercation broke out between a man and a woman. The woman screamed at the man in Italian and ordered the bus driver to stop. The driver pulled over to the side of the road whereupon she got off the bus, still shouting and screaming a tirade of profanities at the man. Everyone craned their necks to get a better look at what was happening, momentarily tearing their eyes away from the television screen. Neither Pat nor I understood enough Italian to work out what the woman was screaming about, but we guessed she'd had her bottom felt too!

Show over, we continued up the winding Via San Domenica. The views over Florence were breathtaking.

It was stifling in the bus as there was no air conditioning, but after about thirty minutes, we finally arrived in the main square,

Piazza Mina, and ground to a halt in front of the Villa Aurora Hotel. We were to meet my prospective employer, Flavia, here. Finding a bench in the piazza we sat down to wait. A few minutes later a shiny black four-wheel-drive vehicle pulled up near us. The driver jumped out of the car and greeted us:

'Buona Sera, Margarita e Patricia?' The woman was dressed immaculately in black matador pants, a crisp white cotton blouse and flat black pumps. Her hair was styled in a fashionable bob and Gucci sunglasses were perched atop her head. She introduced herself.

'Piacere. Sono Flavia'

There was a teenage boy and a pretty, dark-haired young girl in the car. Flavia introduced her son, Luigi and her daughter Giulia. Patricia climbed into the back of the car and Flavia indicated that I should get into the front seat, while telling her son to get out of the car. There was a heated exchange between mother and son and then he just shrugged and walked off. I think she had told him to walk home!

We drove further into the Tuscan hills, along winding roads, until we eventually pulled up in front of some large ornate iron gates. Flavia gave three blasts on the car horn and the gates slid back to reveal the most stupendous villa, possibly eighteenth century. Two servants came running to help us into the house.

Flavia ushered us into her lavishly furnished drawing room. The walls were covered in frescoes of pastoral scenes. Ceiling to floor windows, along the whole length of one wall, opened out onto the garden.

She asked one of the servants to bring tea, which arrived in a large silver teapot on a silver tray, with delicate china cups and saucers and crunchy little almond biscuits. Then the business of the interview began. Flavia wanted an English teacher and chauffeur for her seven-year-old daughter; someone to drive her to school and to social functions. In return, I would have a suite of rooms, use of a car and good remuneration.

Not having a good command of the Italian language, and Flavia not speaking much English, I struggled through the interview with the help of Patricia.

Flavia then walked over to the wall, pushed a button, and a hidden door covered in frescoes sprang open to reveal another part of the villa. She escorted us to the suite of rooms that I would have, which was simply, but tastefully furnished. Her daughter Giulia's bedroom was next door. The villa also included a games room in the basement. Her son, Luigi, was in the room playing a game of pool, so he obviously had managed to hitch a ride home.

Then we ventured into the garden. An ornate fountain played in the lazy afternoon sun. Statues were dotted here and there amongst the shrubbery. The garden sloped down towards the rolling Tuscan hills. In the distance between dark green spears of cypress trees and silver-green olive trees, I could see the terracotta cupola of Santa Maria del Fiore. I caught my breath. My dream come true. I could be living in the Tuscan hills overlooking Florence, just as I had once imagined.

Walking around the garden, a cat crossed our path. Pat made a comment about cats, talking in both English and Italian, and tried to explain to Flavia that she paints and had recently finished an oil painting of cats.

Flavia looked horrified and said they did not use such words.

Puzzled, Pat and I just looked at each other and continued our garden tour. Neither of us understood why she was so upset.

Fortunately, it didn't jeopardise the interview, as I was offered the job there and then. She wanted me to start right away. After explaining that we were on holiday for another week, and I would then have to give at least two weeks' notice to my employer, she said:

'*Va bene*. I will wait for you. Telephone me when you are ready.'

Back at the apartment in Florence, Pat and I discussed what could possibly have upset Flavia when we were in the garden. We concluded that she must have misunderstood and thought Pat was swearing, as *cazzo* (pronounced catso) is an Italian slang word for penis!

At the railway station the following week, en route to the airport for our flight home to London, I saw a woman standing with her back to us looking at the departure board. Her hair was down to her waist. I would have recognised that hair anywhere. I approached her from behind:

'Dawn, is that you?'

She turned around, and indeed it was Dawn, our colleague from the Italian class in London, who'd left for Rome some months ago.

'I don't believe it,' she exclaimed. 'What are you two doing here?'

I explained to her about the interview. Dawn was just on her way back to Rome after visiting friends in Florence.

'Sorry, but I have to go. My train is about to depart. Look, here's my new address.'

She quickly scribbled down an address on a slip of paper and handed it to me.

'If it doesn't work out for you in Florence, come to Rome.'

And with that she dashed off.

* * *

I never needed to hand in my resignation. It was a week after my return to London that the office closed down. I called Flavia in Fiesole to let her know that I would be available to take the job, and to arrange a convenient time for me to start.

'*Non preoccuparti,*' don't worry, she said. 'I have found someone.'

I was stunned. I thought she really wanted me, but obviously she wasn't prepared to wait. *Che sera sera.*

'But if you come to Italy,' she continued, 'I have a friend in Rome you could contact,' whereupon she gave me the address and telephone number of her friend Franca, and we said goodbye.

I now had three contacts in Rome. It was *kismet.*

Bella Roma

Now the 'Fasten Seat Belts' sign is illuminated and the reassuringly mature voice of the pilot, Captain Alex Jamieson, is announcing that we have started our descent and will be landing at Leonardo da Vinci Airport, Fiumicino, in fifteen minutes.

My nerves are getting the better of me, partly from excitement and partly from the impending landing.

I needn't have worried as it's a gentle landing. I breathe a sigh of relief, thankful to be on *terra firma* once more.

Rome!

It seems to take forever to disembark, and even longer for my suitcase to appear on the carousel, which breaks down intermittently. Eventually, I spot it and haul it off the conveyor belt. There are no trolleys in sight, so I wheel it through passport control. My passport doesn't get stamped. I'm disappointed.

I walk through the 'Nothing to Declare' gate and look for *uscita*, the exit. I spot a sign with a picture of a train indicating the direction of the *ferrovia*, railway station. Gayle has advised me to take the train from the airport to Termini Station in the city, as taxis are expensive.

Once in the main terminal of the station, I find the ticket office, *biglietteria*. There is a long queue.

Eventually, I reach the counter. I've been practicing asking for a ticket in Italian.

'*Un biglietto per Termini per favore.*'

'*Andata e ritorno?*' comes the reply. I think he's asking me if I want a return. I hesitate. Suddenly all the Italian I've learned goes out of my head. The young man behind me in the queue comes to my rescue.

'Do you want a return?'

'No, just a single.'

He leans in to the window. '*Andata per favore*,' which now I remember means one way. The ticket clerk fires an amount of lira at me and as I'm not too good with numbers, I hand him a large note. Muttering something under his breath, which I'm sure isn't 'Welcome to Rome', he hands me the ticket and the change.

I thank Sir Galahad behind me and check the departure board. A direct train to Termini is standing on Platform One. There are two very high steps up onto the train and people are struggling to board with their suitcases. I notice that some people, probably the locals, heave their suitcases onto the train first and then board. I do likewise.

The train is packed and luggage is everywhere. Spotting a seat I struggle towards it, but have to leave my suitcase on top of some others in the aisle. A few seconds later, the train departs.

I am sitting opposite a very well-shod lady (I notice the Ferragamos immediately). She is wearing extremely well-cut jeans with a white cotton shirt under a black sweater. The designer black leather loafers on her feet and the obligatory designer sunglasses perched on her head complete the look. So simple, so stylish, so Italian! She is talking on her mobile phone. '*Ah si/certo/tesoro/insieme/sta sera/ciao, ciao, ciao.*' I understand only a few words here and there. I hear lots of English spoken around me, and I get the impression that some of the passengers are expatriates living in Rome, and probably teachers returning for the new school term.

The journey from the airport to Termini takes about half an hour. We've been travelling for about fifteen minutes, through countryside that is not particularly inspiring, when the ticket inspector comes along. I hand over my ticket. He looks at it, then at me, and says something in rapid Italian. I understand only '*non validato*'. I look helplessly at him. I don't know what I've done wrong. The well-shod lady comes to my rescue.

'Eet ees necessary to valeedate zee teecket on zee platform,' she explains in very attractive broken English.

I eye the conductor and murmur, *'Mi dispiace'* feeling like a naughty schoolgirl. I should have validated my ticket in one of the machines situated on the platform before boarding the train. I have only been in Rome for half an hour and already I've broken the rules! The conductor takes pity on this stupid English woman and clips the ticket anyway. Smiling at the well-shod lady I murmur a thousand thanks, *'Grazie mille.'*

Now we are passing through working class suburbs with large grey apartment buildings, and very little vegetation. Derelict buildings and a few isolated farmhouses with red tiled roofs are scattered here and there. We pass an industrial estate. It looks pretty grim. A motorway cuts a swathe through the uninteresting countryside. Graffiti is everywhere but, after all, this is the home of graffiti.

Sometimes the large balloon-like letters are indecipherable. One 'tag' in particular is very prolific; 'ZED' has been very busy. He has a distinctive style and I wonder how long it must have taken him, and how he managed to access some of the places. I imagine him scaling the walls, like a cat burglar during the night, to spray his intricate patterns. On one wall, large inflated letters proclaim 'GRAFFITI PARADISE'!

The train pulls into *Stazione* Termini. I alight from the train and then pull my suitcase off behind me. It seems that we have stopped outside the station, as it takes me about ten minutes to walk down the platform onto the main concourse. It's chaotic. People are trying to board trains before passengers have got off. It's like an obstacle course, and hard work trying to avoid tripping over suitcases that are being pulled along at breakneck speed. There seems to be a sense of panic everywhere!

I spot Gayle amongst the sea of faces waiting at the barrier at the end of the platform. Her familiar wide smile and dusky skin is a welcome sight in the hustle and bustle of the station.

'Hi, Maggie. Welcome to Rome.' She greets me with a hug and a kiss.

It's nearly a year since she stayed with me in London. We've remained in contact on a regular basis. She looks serene and happy.

We are approached by several taxi touts, but Gayle ignores them. Some of them are quite persistent.

'*Va via,*' hisses Gayle. She's told them to get lost!

Walking out of the station the heat hits me like a slap in the face. Securing a licensed taxi, Gayle gives the driver an address in San Giovanni, a south-eastern suburb of Rome. We stop outside a modern, eight-storey apartment building on Via Gallia, a wide tree-lined road. There are green roller shutters at the windows, and each window has a balcony with a profusion of colourful plants in large terracotta pots. Gayle has organised accommodation for me with some of her students until I get myself sorted out. She currently shares an apartment with three male flatmates on the Via dei Capocci in Rioni Monti, an ancient quarter of Rome near the Colosseum.

Pushing a button on the *citofono*—entry-phone—a woman's voice answers, '*Ciao Gayle*,' and the next minute the door clicks open with a buzz. We walk through an inner courtyard into another building opposite and take the lift to the fourth floor.

A petite, pretty, dark-haired girl greets us at the apartment door. Gayle makes the introductions. Ava is Italian and I guess she is in her late twenties. She speaks some English.

The apartment is very spacious. There are five bedrooms, two with private en suite bathrooms and a separate bathroom off the main hall, an eat-in kitchen and a large sitting room. One end of the sitting room has been screened off to form a small study area. In the corner at the other end sits a grand piano. Ava tells me she is studying music at the nearby Academy.

My room is the smallest, but I accept that I'm last in the pecking order and the last one in gets the smallest room. It's not the Ritz, but it's adequate for now. The other three flatmates that I'll be sharing with, all male, are out. Ava is about to go out herself. She hands me a set of keys and says she will see me tomorrow.

I drop my suitcase in my room. There will be ample time later to unpack. Now I want to explore Rome and Gayle is taking me to her favourite pizzeria.

Arm in arm, we walk down Via Gallia, passing a flower stall on the corner. Twinkling fairy lights are draped around a voluminous white canvas awning, used to protect the flowers from the heat of the sun during the day. We continue through an archway of the old Roman city wall, passing a large public park, and into a narrow cobbled street.

It's almost dark now, and as we round the bend at the end of the street I stop dead in my tracks and catch my breath. There, towering above us is the most awe-inspiring sight. The Colosseum. I gasp as I look up at the ancient ruined amphitheatre, the arches now floodlit, a silhouette against the night sky. I will never forget that sight. I'd seen so many pictures of it, but here it was at last, the real thing, and I could touch it!

Nearby at Pizzeria Forum, I watch fascinated as the chefs prepare the pizza bases, working the round flat dough with their hands, sprinkling on the various toppings and then placing them into the large wood-fired oven on their long handled wooden paddles. I eat one of the best pizzas I've ever tasted. It looks huge when it's delivered to the table, but the pastry base is so thin and crispy, I have no trouble in eating every crumb. Mine has a topping of *rugola*, a dark green leaf with a peppery, slightly bitter taste. I've never eaten it before, but it's delicious.

We stroll along the Fiori Imperiale up to Piazza Venezia, passing the ruins of the old Roman Forum, until we arrive at the enormous monument to King Vittorio Emanuele II which completely dominates one end of the piazza. This monument holds the Tomb of the Unknown Soldier. Two guards are on duty at the top of the steps, guarding the eternal flame. Gayle tells me that this monument is also known as the typewriter or the wedding cake, because of its appearance.

Returning along the Fiori Imperiale we finish off the night at Bar Martini where I sit and gaze, enraptured, at the Colosseum towering above us. The dark skinned Arabic-looking waiter introduces himself as Ali Baba. Gayle and I exchange smiles. We catch up on events of the last twelve months. She is teaching English at a private school that has several locations around the city, and is also babysitting to support her work as a scriptwriter and adventurer. Not only has she organised my accommodation, but she has also lined up an interview for me at her school.

'Tomorrow we'll go and see the Principal,' she announces.

When I wake up the following morning, it takes me a few seconds to realise where I am in the unfamiliar surroundings.

The sun streams through the shutters, casting silver strips across the tiled floor. Dust motes dance in the shafts of sunlight. My room faces onto the street and I can hear the flow of early morning traffic and shouts of '*Buongiorno*' as the steel shutters of the shops are raised. I pinch myself. I can hardly believe I'm here.

I slip out of bed, pad along the corridor to the communal bathroom and get my first shock. *Che sciffo!* It's disgusting! I'm sharing this bathroom with two other people and it seems no-one cleans up after themselves. There are dirty footprints in the bath, which has the shower fitted over it, and I need to clean it before I can use it. I shower quickly and return to my room to get dressed for my interview. I feel excited and nervous at the same time.

There doesn't appear to be anyone else in the house, unless they are all still sleeping. I wander along to the kitchen and find that also in a shambles, with pots and pans left dirty in the sink and half-eaten food left on plates, like the abandoned *Mary Celeste*. I cannot face eating here. I decide to have breakfast at the bar next to the apartment block.

The bar is buzzing with people who have stopped for a coffee on their way to work, and the clatter of cups and saucers above the hissing of the coffee machine is deafening. Suddenly, my confidence evaporates, and I'm just about to turn and leave when the *barista* at the coffee machine calls out to me, '*Buongiorno, prego,*' and indicates a table. Returning his smile, I order a *cappuccino e cornetto*. There are several different types of *cornetti*; plain, with chocolate or *con crema*, which is thick, rich custard. Choosing one *con crema* I sit at the table drinking my rather tepid *cappuccino* and watch the comings and goings of the local community.

I notice that customers pay the cashier first, give their ticket to the *barista*, who tears the ticket before serving a small cup of strong black espresso coffee, which customers knock back in one gulp while standing at the bar. It seems to be the custom to leave small change, *spiccioli*, on the counter. Does no one sit, relax and drink their coffee slowly, I wonder? Apparently not, as I find out later, if you sit at a table you pay more.

When I pay at the cash desk before I leave, I'm embarrassed that I've done it back to front. I feel I have tourist written all over me.

I walk down Via Gallia towards the old city wall. Strangers stare at me and wish me '*Buongiorno*'. Do I have *crema* on my face? Or is it the red hair and freckles?

I wait for Gayle at the end of the road, underneath the arch near the flower stall. The vendor keeps giving me the eye.

Gayle arrives breathless some minutes later.

'Hi Maggie,' she greets me with a hug. 'How's the accommodation?'

Not wishing to upset her I say 'Fine.' I'll tell her later.

We take a small orange *autobus* and then the *metro* to Piazza Re di Roma, where the Head Office of the school, Studio Cassino, is situated. Gayle teaches at this school. The *metro* exits onto a large circular park surrounded by drab buildings and shops. The school is situated on the top floor of a large, grey office building on the other side of the road, which encircles the park. An incessant flow of traffic races around the piazza at breakneck speed. Do these Romans think they are in a chariot race? We wait for a break in the traffic and run across the road.

Unscathed, we reach the other side in one piece and enter the office building. The door to the lift has been left open on another floor and it is not operating, so we have to walk up the four flights of stairs to the school.

Gayle introduces me to Antonella, the receptionist, who escorts us to the Principal's office.

The Principal, Nicolas Ottomanelli, is the embodiment of charm; a short, stocky man of about fifty, with steel grey hair and gold-rimmed spectacles. He wears a light grey suit with a black silk shirt, open at the neck to reveal a heavy gold chain. He sports a matching gold chain on his wrist and a gold ring with a single diamond on his little finger. His shoes are loafers of soft black leather. Definitely not the typical school principal.

Sitting in the office is a Catherine Zeta-Jones look-alike. Gayle whispers to me, 'That's Nicolas's mistress, Diana.'

After some preliminaries, I hand Nicolas my CV. He looks at me over the rim of his spectacles, and asks some cursory questions. His hard, dark brown eyes look me up and down. He seems more interested in my legs than in my teaching qualifications and hardly glances at my CV.

He speaks English with a thick Roman accent.

'There is a teaching position available at two different locations, one in Piazza Bologna on Mondays, Tuesdays and Thursdays, and the other at EUR (he pronounces this ay-oor) on Wednesdays and Fridays. It will be fifteen hours a week to start, three hours in the evenings for five evenings. Salary will be 90,000 lire per evening.'

I do a quick calculation. It's about 45 pounds a night at the current exchange rate, which is just over 2,000 lire to the pound sterling. I will be paid in cash fortnightly.

'Are you interested?'

You bet I am. 'Yes, thank you.' I politely reply.

'*Bene, commencia la prossima,*' good, start next week, and with that Nicolas shakes my hand and the interview is terminated.

My legs have obviously passed the test!

The following day I have time to explore the area around the apartment with my guide-book and faithful old camera.

I retrace the route that Gayle and I had taken to the Colosseum, greeting the guy on the flower stall at the end of the road, and walking across Piazzali Metronio, where five or six roads converge into the piazza. There are no markings on the road, so it's a complete free for all. I walk through the archway of the ancient Roman city wall, which I now know is part of the Aurelian Wall, and along Via delle Navicella to the park. I pass through the ornate stone arch, and the imposing Villa Celimontana comes into view. The building now houses the

Geographical Society. Umbrella pine trees—*Pini Romani*—are prolific here. I walk along the gravel pathway under a canopy of aromatic pines and breathe in their intoxicating scent.

At the end of the pathway I find a drinking fountain, which looks like a large fire-hydrant. The cast-iron post and base has turned a dull green colour, but the wolf's head, from whose jaws flows a steady stream of water is a shiny, bright brass. I place my finger over the hole underneath his jaw and a jet of water spurts from a hole on the top of the wolf's head. I bend my head and direct my mouth into the jet, like I've seen some of the locals do. A trickle of water goes into my mouth, but most of it washes over my face and hair. It's a work of art. Drying myself off with a tissue I continue my walk. It seems to be a favourite place for people to bring their dogs and meet up with other canine lovers.

As I walk out of the park, I peer through some railings into the garden of what, I assume, is a gatehouse. In the garden there are numerous cats, all sleeping on old chairs and sofas.

I continue down the tree-lined Via Claudia until I reach the Colosseum. This time it's not floodlit, but it looks just as impressive.

On Via San Giovanni in Laterano is Pizza Forum, an old traditional Neopolitan pizzeria, where I had the tasty pizza with Gayle. I walk to Bar Martini around the corner and say hello to Ali Baba who fusses around me, seats me at a table with an unobstructed view of the Colosseum, and brings me a drink on the house.

Later, returning to Via Gallia, I explore the other end of the street. Halfway up is the rather austere façade of the Chiesa di Nativita, The Church of the Nativity. The door is open so I peek inside. The altar is an unusual circular shape with an alcove behind that is covered in rich mosaics of Mary, Joseph, Jesus and the three Kings.

Tip-toeing quietly inside, I pop a coin in the box marked *Offerte*. In front of the altar I admire an octagonal marble centrepiece with inlaid stained glass panels depicting the nativity. There's not another soul in the church as far as I can tell, so when the organ springs to life, its music resounding around the church, it startles me. It's surreal, and I feel like I'm in a scene from *Phantom of the Opera*!

Further up the street is Bar Enoteca, a *pasticceria* and *cioccolatoria*. The windows display all types of sweet biscuits and chocolates. The *bocconcini alla mandorla* makes my mouth water and I'd really like to buy some, but I'm too shy to enter the shop.

Later, at the apartment, I meet my three other flatmates; Ava's brother Mario, Rafael, who is half Italian and half English and Niall who is German. They are all students and almost half my age.

I suddenly wonder, 'What am I doing here?'

When arriving in Italy you must register with the police within eight days, and for a stay of more than three months you must obtain a *Permesso di Soggiorno*, permit of stay.

Obtaining a *Permesso di Soggiorno* can be a very long-winded process. You must apply in person to the *Questura*, the Police Headquarters on Via Genova, which can be more than a little daunting. Italians love a uniform and undergo a complete personality change when wearing one. The bureaucratic red tape is endless, extremely excessive, and can be very frustrating.

A number of documents must be produced. I need to obtain and complete an application form from the Post Office, and a *Marca da Bollo,* a tax stamp that looks like a postage stamp, which is a stamp duty fee for the processing of the documents. I have to provide my passport, four identical passport size photographs of myself and proof of my address while in Rome, along with evidence that I can support myself. I also need a certificate of fitness, which I had obtained from my doctor before I left London.

I arrive at the *Questura* the following morning just after eight o'clock. There is already a line of people outside the main entrance.

After about half an hour the line starts to move very slowly. Another twenty minutes later an officer informs us that only ten people can be processed and they have had their quota for the day. He proceeds to close the doors. We are told to come back tomorrow. I thought he was going to get lynched! The officials had left us standing in line for almost an hour, knowing that only ten people were allowed in.

The next morning I return at seven o'clock and already there is a queue, but I'm relieved to find myself about eighth in line. Eventually, I'm allowed inside the building and called to a *sportello,* a window at the counter, where an officer is sitting behind a glass partition. I hand over my documents and photographs to him and, with a frown on his face, he painstakingly peruses everything. I notice his name badge—Antonio—he's rather dishy. When he sees my teaching certificate amongst the documents his manner becomes more amiable. His son, he tells me, is in London studying English. He leaves the window with my application form in his hand and retreats to an inner office. I'm left wondering if there is a problem.

After what seems an interminable amount of time, during which I'm hopping impatiently from one foot to the other, Antonio returns to the desk and asks me to sign a paper that has my photograph stapled to it. It's my *Permesso di Soggiorno Per Stranieri,* which states that I am domiciled in Rome to work as an *insegnante,* a teacher. Picking up his rubber stamp, Antonio brings it down hard on the paper several times and then, with a flourish, hands me the document and bids me *'Buona fortuna!'*

Now I have to obtain a *Codice Fiscale,* equivalent to a National Insurance number in the UK. The Agenzia Entrata office is in Ottaviano, near the Vatican. I walk up to Termini and take the A-line *metro.*

Compared to obtaining my *Permesso,* the procedure is easy, although I spend most of the afternoon there. I produce my passport and my permit to stay and then I am given a card with a personalised sixteen-digit number on it. Now I am legal to work.

I take the opportunity to organise my *tessera,* a travel card that will allow me to travel on the buses and the *metro.* It costs 50,000 lire and is valid for one month. These can be obtained from Termini Station, or from any shop that has the *Tabacchaio* symbol displayed, a white letter 'T' on a black background. I have to try three before I can find one that has a *tessera*, the other two having sold out. This was to be a regular occurrence. I also purchase some *francobolli*, postage stamps, and two *cartoline*, postcards, just to practice my Italian.

When the shopkeeper hands me the change, he also gives me a wrapped sweet. 'How nice,' I think. However, when I check my change I realise that it's wrong, and with my limited Italian, I start to protest. *'Sbagliato,'* I mutter, pointing out that he has made a mistake, quickly placing the change back on the counter. He shrugs and fires a string of Italian words at me. I understand that he's telling me he has no change. He picks up the money from the counter and starts counting it into my hand, placing the sweet into my hand at the final count, instead of a coin.

I learn from Gayle later that this is normal practice, as small change, for some reason, is scarce, and so if there are no small coins to make up a customer's change, you receive a sweet!

Termini Station is Rome's mainline railway station and the interchange for the underground public transport system, the *Metropolitana*. There are two lines: A (orange) and B (blue). Attempts to build extra lines come to a halt when excavations reveal ancient ruins. It is a continual work in progress. Termini is also the *capolinea*, terminus, for the buses and main railway network.

The skies above Termini are swarming with starlings. In the autumn, millions of these birds arrive from Northern Europe. They amass in the Roman pine trees in the area, an ideal roosting place. Intermittently, and in unison, as if by some secret signal, they fly out of the trees swooping and circling overhead. The cacophony is deafening and walking through Termini becomes an assault course trying to dodge the droppings from the birds. It's normal to use an umbrella while in the area as a precaution, and the smell of excrement is quite pungent.

Seen from a distance, the flocks of birds appear as plumes of smoke, creating a formation of constantly changing patterns in a mesmerising aerial display. It is a phenomenon that has to be seen to be believed.

On Thursdays the area is also filled with Filipino women who are employed as domestic help. It's a meeting place to catch up with friends and relatives, and to hear the latest news from home. It's also the grapevine as to who is looking for help, and operates like an employment agency. Most of the employers here in Rome give their domestic help Thursday afternoons off, whether by chance or by design, I have yet to find out.

I arrange to meet Gayle at Termini a couple of evenings later.

'There's someone I'd like you to meet,' she says mysteriously.

She arrives with a strikingly good-looking man. He is tall and slim, with an aquiline nose and a sensual mouth. She introduces him to me as Francesco. He and I have an immediate rapport. Italian born, he speaks excellent English with an American accent.

When I compliment him on his English he bristles with pride.

Frankie, as he prefers to be called, is an actor. Gayle met him at acting classes and they became firm friends. Sometimes he works as a film extra at the Cinecitta film studios in Rome. His film work is very sporadic, and although acting is his passion, he cannot make a decent living from that alone, and so he also teaches English at EUR, one of the schools where I will be teaching.

I'm beginning to wonder if everyone here needs two jobs to survive!

We all jump on the bus to Trastevere, a medieval quarter of Rome, situated across the River Tiber. The bus shakes and rattles over the cobblestones. The seats are wooden and the vibration goes through our bodies. Gayle and I are enjoying the ride. It puts a smile on our faces. As we are waiting to get off the bus before it pulls into Largo Argentina, other passengers jostle and try to push past us. One woman is breathing down my neck. '*Scendi qui?*' she asks. Frankie turns around, says '*Sì*' then looks at me and rolls his eyes. Several other people are asking, '*Scendi qui la prossima?*' The question is passed down the bus like a Chinese whisper. They're asking if we're getting off the bus at the next stop. Frankie starts to mimic *sotto voce*, asking Gayle and I, '*Scendi qui?*' making us laugh.

Rome has an efficient tram network so we take the tram from Largo Argentina to Piazza Sonnino in Trastevere.

Wandering through the labyrinth of narrow cobbled streets, we arrive at Piazza Santa Maria in Trastevere. The church in the piazza has beautiful gilded mosaics on the façade. It's closed, but I make a mental note to come back and explore. The steps of a large fountain in the centre of the piazza are a resting place for locals and tourists, and around the piazza there are bars and restaurants with tables and chairs outside. It's a wonderful atmosphere.

From the piazza we turn down a narrow alley to Cinema Pasquino, which shows English films. Paying the 5,000 lire entrance fee at the cash desk, we part the heavy, red velvet drapes that substitute as doors, and enter the theatre. It's surprisingly large inside. We settle down on the rather uncomfortable seats to watch *Jurassic Park,* a Steven Spielberg movie. Suddenly, I hear a loud whirring and grating sound from above. I look up to see the roof of the cinema sliding open, and there we sit watching the movie beneath the starry Roman sky!

After the movie we have a pizza at the Roma Sparita Restaurant in the nearby Piazza Santa Cecilia. At the end of the meal, we are given small glasses containing a sweet, sticky, citrus-based lemon liqueur, called *limoncello*. It's normal practice to take this after a meal as a digestive. I grimace as I taste it, and Gayle and Frankie both laugh.

'Don't you just *love* it, Margarita?' Frankie says pursing his lips, but I notice he hasn't touched his at all.

We leave the restaurant and stroll leisurely around the warren of alleyways, beneath a canopy of washing-lines that are strung across the narrow streets. Colourful flowers cascade from tiny balconies. It's enchanting.

Later, we stop for a while at Blatumba, a piano bar, where a Spanish guitarist serenades us with flamenco music. It's almost midnight now and Gayle and Frankie decide to call on their friend Heather. When she doesn't answer the intercom, Gayle and Frankie stand on the street outside her *palazzo* calling her name. 'HEATHERRR! HEATHERRR!' When she appears at her open window on the top floor, wet-haired from the shower, they conduct a very loud conversation with her from the street. I feel embarrassed because it's very late, and I fully expect neighbouring windows to be flung open and to be told in no uncertain terms to shut-up, but apparently this method of calling on people is normal practice, and accepted.

Promising to catch up with her another time, we take the bus back to Termini and all go our separate ways.

'Ciao bella,' calls Frankie. 'See you in EUR next week.'

I turn to Gayle.

'I really do like him,' I admit.

She looks at me with that all knowing, all wise look of hers, and surprises me by saying, 'Out of bounds honey, he's gay.'

You could have knocked me down with a feather. Okay, I had thought on a couple of occasions he was being a bit of a drama queen, but I put that down to him being an actor.

I'm incredulous. 'No, I'd never have guessed it. Maybe all he needs is the love of a good woman.'

'It won't work,' she laughs. 'But he did kiss me once after he'd bragged that he was a good kisser and I asked him to show me.'

'Well, and was he?' I ask, feeling just a tinge of jealousy.

'Oh, sure,' she answers flippantly.

I'm disappointed, but, for the time being, I have to be content with Frankie as a friend, although inwardly I'm already scheming to get him straightened out!

The English Teacher

I feel quite nervous. It's my first day of teaching at the school in Piazza Bologna. Like Piazza Re di Roma, Piazza Bologna is a large circular island park. Around the piazza there are shops, cafes, bars and office buildings. This piazza appears to be more upmarket than Re di Roma. Businessmen sit reading *Il Corriere* or *La Stampa* newspapers. Young mothers or nannies stroll with their children. *Signore* walk their dogs and the *anziani,* elderly, amble around with their young companions.

The gardens are well kept, with flowerbeds and leafy trees that afford some shade. A little bar is tucked away in the corner of the garden, with a few tables and chairs placed under a vine-covered pergola.

I arrive early for my lesson, so I have a *cappuccino* (another lukewarm one) at the bar and then stroll around the gardens. One of the flower beds has a large clock face made out of flowers and a memorial plaque, with an inscription in Italian. I work out in my not-so-good Italian that a magistrate, Giovanni Falcone, and his wife were assassinated on 23 May 1992 at 17:08. The hands of the flower clock depict this time. I feel a slight chill down my spine.

Later I find out that Falcone, his wife and three bodyguards were killed by a Mafia henchman's roadside bomb as they drove outside Palermo in Sicily.

Falcone was anti-Mafia and responsible for putting several *Mafioso* behind bars.

He specialised in prosecuting the Sicilian Casa Nostra and once said: 'He who's afraid dies every day. Who's not afraid, dies only once'.

As I walk along Via Livorno on my way from the Piazza to the school, I notice a shop set back from the street in a small courtyard, which has Torrefazione written in gold letters above the front window. It advertises *Dolciumi Vari, Caramelle/ Cioccalato*. I'm curious, so I have a quick look inside. The shop is tiny, but crammed with chocolates, sweets in large jars, hessian sacks full of coffee beans and lots of other goodies. I can't resist, and purchase a few chocolates, choosing them individually from the glass case at the counter. The shop assistant starts to gift-wrap my small purchase, and when I try to explain that they are for me and not a gift, saying, '*Non e un regalo*' she just smiles, continues wrapping, then hands me the beautifully wrapped package.

My students at Piazza Bologna are young adults, both male and female, aged between eighteen and thirty. They are enthusiastic, respectful and good fun.

Although I have a lesson plan, it goes right out of the window and the lesson becomes a spontaneous, lively discussion. We cover many topics from politics to popular music and, amazingly, the students are word perfect when it comes to British song lyrics.

At the end of the lesson, they all appear to have enjoyed themselves. I leave the school feeling very relieved and very pleased with myself.

On Tuesday I arrive early at the school and Christina, the receptionist, is talking on the telephone at the desk. She appears extremely agitated and is practically hyperventilating.

When she sees me she looks immensely relieved and slams down the receiver. Apparently, one of the teachers hasn't turned up and she has been unable to find a substitute teacher. She pleads with me to take the class. It will be forty-five minutes now as fifteen minutes of the hour has already gone. It would turn out to be the longest forty-five minutes I've ever known.

I agree to take the lesson and sally forth into the classroom, where there are a dozen children running amok. I guess their ages range from four to twelve. *Madonna!* What have I let myself in for?

Walking to my desk, I proceed to take out my books and resolutely place them on the table in front of me. A hush falls over the classroom. I then eyeball one of the older girls and ask her to come and clean the blackboard. I have no lesson plan and I am totally unprepared to teach a class of kids. Back to basics!

I'm in the middle of asking the kids to introduce themselves, when there is a knock on the door and in walks Christina, followed by a young boy and a woman who, I guess, is his mother.

Christina seats the boy at a desk, his mother bills and coos over him and then, much to his dismay, she leaves. He looks terrified and starts to cry. My Italian isn't good enough to be able to console him. One of the older boys quietly talks to him, and eventually the child stops crying. I continue the lesson, asking simple questions to assess the level of the class. They are all at different levels. The small boy, whose name I eventually manage to extract from him is Manuel, will not participate at all.

Suddenly one of the girls starts to giggle and whispers something to her friend, who glances over at Manuel, and she also starts to giggle. Before I can ask them why they are laughing, they point to the floor beneath Manuel's chair. There is a puddle on the floor. He has wet his pants! Cursing his absent mother for dumping him on me (I'm probably cheaper than a babysitter), I do my best to reassure him and take him outside to the reception area, explain the problem to Christina and ask her to telephone the boy's mother to come and collect him. Christina returns to the classroom armed with rolls of tissues and proceeds to mop up the pee.

I resume the lesson and all goes well for another fifteen minutes or so, when suddenly pandemonium breaks out. Some of the little monsters are screaming and jumping onto their chairs. One of them points to a little furry creature scurrying across the floor. It's a mouse. I want to jump onto a chair myself, but when the mouse reaches the wall it stops. It's a wind-up toy.

Angelic looking twin girls, Alessandra and Francesca, aged about ten are red in the face from trying not to laugh. They admit the mouse is theirs. The little angels have turned into little devils.

For the second time since I arrived in Rome, I ask myself, 'What am I doing here?'

Trying to keep my cool, I ask one of the girls to bring the mouse to me, whereupon it sits on my desk for the remainder of the lesson, which is all about *il topo*, the mouse!

The kids love the lesson, but as far as I'm concerned it's the first, and last time, I will teach children. However, when the lesson is over, Alessandra, who seems to be the ringleader of the two, approaches me, flings her arms around me and kisses me. Nevertheless, I'm relieved to get back to my mature students.

EUR lies on the southern edge of Rome. It's an ugly suburb, built by the Fascist dictator, Benito Mussolini, in the 1930s. It was originally intended as the *Exposizione Universale di Roma*, to hold the International Exhibition of 1942, which never materialised due to the outbreak of World War II. The only compensation is the Viale Europa, a wide tree-lined boulevard with upmarket shops, bars, and restaurants.

When I arrive around six o'clock on Wednesday, lots of people are milling around. The evening *passeggiata*—the ritual of walking before dinner—has begun.

The school is situated on the Via Tupini, in one of the few remaining beautiful old buildings that were spared when Mussolini built the new town. In the grounds of the building a fountain in a central courtyard is surrounded by lush tropical shrubbery.

The classrooms are light and airy, but apart from a blackboard, a desk and a few chairs, the room is empty. I have a lot of material for which I need an overhead projector and have to beg Angela, the receptionist, to organise one for me. It doesn't materialise. Frankie is teaching in the next classroom. He not only has an overhead projector, but also a television and video recorder. I borrow his projector, and add TV and video recorder to my requisition.

I've been looking forward to teaching in EUR and seeing Frankie again. After school, we walk through the nearby park. At the edge of a large artificial lake a restaurant sits on stilts in the water. We sit on the deck and, over a beer, watch the ducks and boats before heading back to Termini. Frankie tells me he is making a short movie and will not be teaching for the next couple of weeks.

I still find him very attractive.

On Thursday I am awoken by a loud clap of thunder. The windows rattle. I jump out of bed and open the shutters, just as a spectacular flash of lightning streaks across the sky. A few large drops of rain have plopped onto the pavement below. Another, even louder, clap of thunder encourages me to close the windows. Just in time, as next minute the rain is lashing against them.

The streets are flooded and the public transport system is totally disrupted. It's a fiasco. I telephone the school at Piazza Bologna to cancel my lessons. The storm lasts for six hours. I'm marooned *in casa*.

At EUR on Friday I've been allocated an overhead projector, but no TV and video. Angela assures me that I will have them for next week.

When my class has finished a very smart, mature lady approaches me.

'I would like to join your class,' she tells me. 'I am at the moment in the class of Frankie.'

I'm a little surprised. 'Why do you want to change?'

'I've heard that you are a good teacher and I am bored of owls.'

I'm puzzled. 'Why are you bored with owls?'

'Because we have learned about owls for six lessons and I am now boring.'

I wonder if she has perhaps made a mistake with her vocabulary and ask her to say owls in Italian.

'*Gufi!*' she exclaimed.

Which indeed, does mean owls, but I'm still baffled why Frankie would spend six lessons teaching that subject.

'Alright, I'll speak to Frankie and next week you can come to my lesson.'

Frankie would be making his movie anyway, so his class

would have a substitute teacher. It would be an ideal time for this student to join my class.

'What's your name?' I ask her.

'Luana,' she replies. *'Grazie mille.'*

I didn't know then that we would become good friends and one day she would save my life.

Over the next couple of weeks Frankie is making his movie and Gayle is assisting him, so I don't see them at all. Then an invitation to the premiere showing of his film arrives in the mail. On the evening of the show Gayle and I take the bus together to the Grauco Cinema on Via Perugia, a lively and interesting film club dedicated to lesser-known independent cinema. It's a full house. Three films are being shown, all short independent movies, and the winner will receive an award.

Frankie's movie opens with a surreal phantom-like scene as two dancers, a male and female, dance to the music of *O Fortuna*, a movement from the Opera *Carmina Burana* by the German composer Carl Orff, along with *Don't Cry for Me Argentina* sung by Sinead O'Connor. There is no dialogue in the film.

It's a spectacular performance, very professionally directed, and the choreography is superb. I'm very impressed.

Obviously the audience is too, judging from the applause. The movie is entitled *The Immortal Kiss*.

When I see Frankie at school in EUR the following week, I tell him that Luana has transferred to my class. He seems very distracted and excited about something, and is hardly listening to me. When I explain that Luana was bored, learning about owls for six weeks, he makes a strangulated noise, shrugs and rolls his eyes. I come to the conclusion that he is totally burnt out and has lost all interest in teaching.

Suddenly he puts his arms around me and squeezes me tightly.

'Guess what?' My film has won first prize!' He's over the moon.

Later that night we meet up with Gayle in the centre and celebrate with a drink at the Why Not pub near the Pantheon.

Piazza Navona

Gayle has made friends with several people of different nationalities since arriving in Rome. Many of them are refugees from war-torn Yugoslavia. Their gathering place is in the beautiful Piazza Navona, an oval-shaped piazza with lots of bars and restaurants and a bustling nightlife.

Artists gather in the piazza to sell their paintings to the never-ending stream of tourists, and it is here that I meet Alessandro, one of the artists.

From the moment I first set eyes on him I know that this man will be special to me. He is tanned, has dark curly hair, high cheekbones and a Roman nose. His slightly hooded 'come-to-bed' eyes are like dark, deep pools, drawing me in. I feel like I am drowning.

Gayle and I pause to look at some of his work. The oil paintings are excellent; bold and colourful. I note his signature on the paintings is Alessandro. I've found my Botticelli!

We exchange a few words. His English is limited and I struggle with my Italian. After a few minutes Gayle and I move on.

I can't get him out of my mind. My head is filled with fantasies of walking hand in hand with him across the piazza to his studio, which surely must be nearby.

> *He takes my hand and we walk across the piazza, down a narrow cobble-stoned backstreet until we reach his studio.*
>
> *It's a typical artist's studio, big and airy, with lots of light. A large easel with a blank canvas stands in the corner, waiting for him to create a work of art, a masterpiece, maybe a portrait of me? I pose for him. He picks up his brushes and works quietly at the canvas.*

> *Eventually, our passions overcome us and he throws down his brushes, gathers me in his arms and carries me to his unmade bed. The musky scent of his body still lingers on the sheets. He's like a wild animal, and as he undresses me his breathing becomes harder. We make mad passionate love and fall into a deep sleep in each other's arms, satiated, as the first rays of light peek through the shutters...*

Gayle's voice interrupts my thoughts, dragging me from my reverie.

'Hey, wake up Maggie!' She smiles. She knows exactly what I'm dreaming about.

In reality, although Gayle and I occasionally go to the piazza on our way home from school, we hardly speak to Alessandro, partly because of the language barrier, and partly because he is always surrounded by people, although he always acknowledges us.

It's Halloween. Gayle, Frankie and I are invited to a party by some American friends from their acting class. It will be held in one of the fabulous hilltop villas in Castel Gandolfo, one of the Castelli Romani towns, about thirty kilometres from Rome.

Heather has also been invited, so we all meet up at her house in Trastevere before the party, to raid her dressing-up box.

Frankie is wearing his black cloak with the red lining and has grown fangs. Heather dresses as a sexy red devil. Gayle is the wicked witch, complete with pointed hat and broomstick, and I am an American Indian Chief with a feathered headdress. It's not quite in keeping with the theme of Halloween, but it looks fantastic. It's also very heavy.

We set off in Heather's car, attracting more than a few stares along the way. It's dark by the time we arrive at the party and it takes us some time to find the entrance to the villa, which is well hidden behind dense shrubbery and a high wooden fence. On entering the gates, a long driveway stretches before us lined with Jack-o-Lanterns, pumpkins with carved out eyes, nose and mouth, and candles burning inside, giving them an eerie glow in the dark. There are life-size ghoulish figures hiding in the shrubbery, and one is hanging from a tree by his neck. Two legs protrude from the garden well. Nearby, in a small 'graveyard', hands reach out of the ground grasping at the air, while a mummified corpse pushes open the lid of its coffin. Spooky!

The house itself is a beautiful rambling old villa and there are about a hundred guests moving between the house and the garden, most of them dressed for the occasion. It's all very theatrical and I find it quite fascinating.

Halloween is not celebrated in England. We celebrate Guy Fawkes' Night, which falls shortly after Halloween on the fifth of November. Guy Fawkes plotted to blow up the Houses of Parliament in 1605, but his plan was foiled and he was sent to the gallows. It became known as The Gunpowder Plot. Every year on the fifth of November effigies of Guy Fawkes are burnt on bonfires around the country amidst firework displays.

Similarly in Italy, Halloween is not celebrated. *Ognissanti*, All Saints' Day, is celebrated on the first of November.

We finally leave the party just before sunrise. On the way home we make a detour past Lake Albano, stop the car on the road at the bottom of a hill, and all pile out. Frankie opens the boot of the car and takes out some empty tin cans which he proceeds to roll down the road. I wonder if he's lost his marbles, then gasp in amazement as the tin cans roll back up to us. We've stopped at the incredible gravity backwards hill.

'A different language is a different vision of life' said Federico Fellini.

I love living in this Eternal city. I love the language, the food, the wine, the whole atmosphere. I love the warm idyllic autumn evenings, known as *Ottobrate Romane*, teaching at Piazza Bologna or EUR and meeting up with Gayle and Frankie. Often Frankie and I walk through the park near the school and stop at the restaurant overlooking the lake for a drink or a pizza.

Most weekends the three of us meet up and take the bus to Trastevere and wander around the narrow, picturesque lanes, stopping for lunch at a pizzeria.

We love the movies and regularly go to Pasquino cinema.

Often the movie breaks down, but no one seems to mind. It's an opportune moment to pop out and buy a *gelato*, or a cold drink as there is no air conditioning in the cinema, except for the sliding roof!

After the movie, we walk into Piazza di Santa Maria in Trastevere and stop at one of the bars to 'people watch' as the evening *passeggiata* commences. It's really like a fashion parade, with the aim being to see and be seen.

I soon adopt this ritual myself as I find it an extremely civilised way to spend an hour before dinner. Not for the Italians a bar for pre-dinner drinks. They prefer to drink their wine with their meal. Young children are given diluted wine with their evening meal, and I really believe that's why there is no binge drinking amongst teenagers here. They've grown up with wine, so it's no big deal.

Children regularly accompany their parents to restaurants. It's real quality time for most families. The *bambini* are, on the whole, extremely well-behaved, and in the summer months dine with their parents into the late evening.

When I remark on the fact that the children are kept up late, I'm told that because of the hot weather the children do not sleep early anyway, as many apartments do not have air-conditioning.

Gelaterie in Italy are as popular as wine bars in England. It's not unusual for young couples on a date to go to a *gelateria* for an ice cream. I find it rather endearing.

Other evenings Gayle, Frankie and I meander around the *centro storico,* historic centre, usually finishing off the night in Piazza Navona. If Alessandro isn't too busy I stop for a while to talk to him. He always seems pleased to see me, and although there is still a language barrier, the eyes say it all. I feel there is some strong chemistry between us. Or is it wishful thinking?

One evening when I pass through the piazza on my way home from school, Alessandro is talking to an attractive blonde woman. A young boy and a dog are playing nearby. I wonder if it's his wife and son. Maybe he's a family man. I pretend I haven't seen him and keep a low profile.

It's my birthday. I'm teaching at Piazza Bologna this evening. I don't mention to my students that it's my birthday. The lesson, as usual, takes its own course and the three hours just fly by.

I'm putting away my books after the lesson and one of my students, Stefano, who is real eye-candy, is hanging around. When the other students have left the classroom he hands me a package.

'What is it Stefano?'

'Open it and see,' he smiles mysteriously.

I tear off the wrapping paper to reveal a box with a cellophane lid, through which I can see an exotic orchid.

'What's the occasion?' I ask.

He smiles. 'Did you tink I would not remember your birfday?' (My students have a problem to pronounce 'th').

During one of our first lessons we discussed zodiac signs and discovered that both he and I are Scorpio, my birthday falling a week before his.

Thanking him, I plant a kiss on his cheek. I'm touched that he's remembered.

Later, I meet up with Frankie and Gayle in Trastevere for a celebratory dinner. Pasquino are showing *The Age of Innocence* with my favourite actor, Daniel Day-Lewis, so we decide to see it before eating. Gayle brings along a fellow American called Chris whom she'd met at a party a few months previously. We have a very pleasant evening at Roma Sparita, and Chris buys a bottle of bubbly to toast my birthday while they all sing '*Tanti auguri*', Happy birthday.

Chris tells me that he came to Rome to work for IBM for twelve months and fell in love with the city. He decided to stay on when his contract expired and set up his own, very successful computer business.

Born into a musical family, he joined the Giulia Cappella Choir of Rome and sings as a soloist in St Peter's Basilica and the Pantheon. As Gayle puts it, 'he has golden pipes.' Chris has lovely, liquid-brown eyes, which remind me of a spaniel puppy. I find him very *simpatico*.

When we leave the restaurant, he asks for my phone number, which he enters into his mobile phone.

I spend most of the following day nursing a giant-sized hangover. Later that evening I receive a telephone call from Chris inviting me out next Saturday, which I accept.

On Saturday Chris picks me up in his green Ford convertible.

'I want to show you something,' he says.

We take the Aventine Hill, climbing higher and higher until we reach the Piazza Cavalieri di Malta—The Square of the Knights of Malta—where the Knight's Priory is situated, the headquarters of this religious order. Although the Priory is closed to the public, the gardens are open and a group of people are gathered in front of a large wooden gate that bars the entrance to the Priory. They are lining up to look through an ornate circular keyhole in the door.

Chris won't tell me what it is they are looking at, as he wants it to be a surprise. I'm in suspense. When it's my turn, I peek through the keyhole, and in the distance, through a long tunnel of mingling tree branches, is a perfectly framed picture postcard view of St Peter's Basilica. Amazing!

Later that evening we drive to Prati, a middle-class suburb that boasts fine restaurants and nightclubs, where we have dinner and listen to jazz at Alexander Platz nightclub. I enjoy Chris's company and we arrange to meet up again soon.

The following evening I go alone to Piazza Navona. It's quite late and I don't know if Alessandro will still be there. He is, but he's talking to some people. I wait until he's alone and then approach him.

When he sees me he moves towards me and a smile spreads over his face. He looks happy to see me. *'Ciao bella,'* he says. The words make me go weak at the knees as he kisses me on both cheeks, his hands putting gentle pressure on my upper arms. I feel myself blushing and I'm glad it's dark.

I spend some time talking to him, and get the feeling that he wants to say something but maybe can't find the words in English.

I walk around the piazza for a while and then saunter casually back over to Alessandro to say, *'Ciao.'*

'*Ciao, a piu tardi,*' he calls after me. He hopes to see me soon. I hope so too. I leave the Piazza and feel that all my birthdays have come at once.

The Fountains of Rome

'Marble and water—the two luxury objects of Rome!' So wrote Edmond About in 1859.

I love the fountains of Rome. Apparently there are about 1000 of them! Gayle and I spend a whole day photographing as many as we can. My favourite and one of the most exquisite is the *Fontane delle Tartarughe*, Fountain of the Turtles, which graces Piazza Mattei in the Ghetto. Four naked youths each stand on the head of a bronze dolphin, their arms outstretched to a turtle perched precariously on a basin high above their heads, while a gentle trickle of water washes over their torsos from the overflowing basin above them.

We hear the steady roar of water before we arrive at the Piazza di Trevi. Entering the piazza, the fountain is an awe-inspiring sight.

The *Fontana di Trevi* became famous because of the films *Three Coins in the Fountain* and *La Dolce Vita*, of Fellini fame. In *La Dolce Vita* Anita Ekberg jumps into the water, fully clothed, and then invites Marcello Mastroianni to join her. I wonder if I jump in will a 'Marcello' join me.

The legend says that if you want to return to Rome you must throw in a coin. However, you must stand with your back to the fountain, hold the coin in your right hand and throw it into the water over your left shoulder, while making your wish. If you throw in two coins you will meet an Italian man. Three coins will ensure that you marry him! Gayle and I throw in a coin. A sudden gust of wind blows a drizzle of spray over us and we run up the steps, giggling like schoolgirls, to the nearby *gelateria*.

One of the most beautiful fountains must surely be *La Fontana delle Quattro Fiumi*, sculpted by Bernini, which dominates the centre of Piazza Navona. Four allegorical figures supporting an obelisk represent the four continents, Europe, Asia, Africa and America and the four rivers of the world, the Danube, Ganges, Nile, and Rio de la Plata.

At the south end of the Piazza is the *Fontana del Moro* and at the north end is the *Fontana di Nettuno*.

In Piazza Barberini the Baroque *Fontana di Triton*, another beautiful fountain, also sculpted by Bernini, depicts the figure of Triton, half man, half fish, sitting upon a gigantic open clam shell, blowing a jet of water to the sky from a conch shell.

No-one need go thirsty in Rome. There are fountains everywhere. Usually the water is fresh spring water. The prolific small drinking-water fountains, *fontanelle,* look similar to a large fire hydrant, and water flows continuously from a spout. The Italians call these *nasone* which means big nose, because the curved water pipe resembles a giant curved nose!

I am so inspired by the fountains that I write a poem. It's the first of many about my experiences in Rome.

After teaching during the week and most weekends, Gayle and I invariably end up in Piazza Navona for a coffee or a glass of wine, at one of the bars or restaurants which surround the piazza.

Sometimes we decide to walk home along the Fiori Imperiale towards the Colosseum to our apartments. Usually, we haven't got very far before a car pulls up alongside us and the driver calls out '*Dov'e vai*?' Where are you going? Would you like a ride?

Occasionally, we graciously accept the offer and off we go with a complete stranger. It never occurs to either of us that we might be in danger as we feel completely safe in Rome. We are both responsible, mature women, and would not have accepted a ride if we had felt in the least bit threatened. We certainly would not have done it in America or England, but this is the strange thing about Rome, it makes you behave in ways completely out of character. We do have a rule that we accept a lift only when the driver is alone and we always stay together. We trust our instincts.

Sometimes these knights in shining armour take Gayle

and I straight home, chiding us for walking alone so late, as if responsible for our safety.

Other times we agree to go for a spin around the city or drive up the hill to Gianicolo, a belvedere over the city and a renowned spot for lovers. We park the car in the small piazza, overlooked by the enormous equestrian statue of the legendary Guiseppe Garibaldi, the Italian military and political leader who led the *Risorgimento*, the political and social movement for the unification of Italy. With his thousand men, known as the Red Shirts, Garibaldi helped free the Italians from foreign rule and unify the country in the nineteenth century. In the nearby gardens, pathways are lined with numerous stone busts of the patriots of Garibaldi.

From a low stone wall in the piazza, we drink in the breathtaking view of Rome by night, with the lights of the city twinkling below us. The Vittorio Emanuele Monument is clearly visible in the distance, dominating the skyline, all shiny and white.

One night Gayle and I make a *passeggiata* a little way down the hill from the piazza and discover the magnificent bronze equestrian monument of Anita Garibaldi. She is seated on a horse, which is mid-stride, her hair flying in the breeze and her right arm is raised above her head brandishing a pistol. I gasp in disbelief, for in her other arm she carries her child!

I stand for a long time gazing at this statue. Brazilian born, Anita left her husband to join Garibaldi as his companion in arms, and later became his lover and wife.

Such passion. She died at thirty-nine fighting for her beliefs. There was a woman to be reckoned with!

I've always liked big flashy sports cars, so when the red low-slung sports job with prancing horse emblem—yes it was a Ferrari—pulls up alongside Gayle and I on the Fiori Imperiale one night and the young, dark haired driver offers us a ride, we hesitate only momentarily.

We squeeze into the car behind the driver and his friend (some rules are made to be broken) who introduce themselves as Filippo and Francesco. I have my eye on the driver, Filippo.

We roar off into the night, through the streets of Rome, heading north and finally screech to a halt outside one of the most exclusive nightclubs in the city. When Filippo gets out of the car, I'm dismayed that he is much shorter than me. Trying not to show my disappointment, we all go into the nightclub. I'm hoping he won't expect me to dance with him as I tower above him. Of course, he does, but sensing my reluctance, suggests that I take off my shoes. That would have been fine but for the fact that I am wearing trousers which now drag the floor, hampering my dancing. Filippo excuses himself and disappears. That's that, I think to myself, I've been dumped, but after a couple of minutes he returns with a handful of pins, gets down on his knees and proceeds to pin up the bottom of my trousers! We dance all night.

Gayle and I often go to the Via Veneto, a wide road lined with plane trees, and stop for cocktails at The Café de Paris that advertises itself as *Il Caffè della dolce vita* and try to imagine what life was like in *la dolce vita* of the 1960s. Along the Via Veneto there are many luxurious hotels, restaurants and Ministry buildings. Sometimes we walk up to the Hard Rock Cafe, situated opposite the heavily guarded American Embassy, or continue on to Harry's Bar.

It is here, one evening after school, that Gayle and I meet Francesco, a prosperous looking guy from Milan on a business trip to Rome. He insists on buying us a drink and then invites us to a nearby nightclub with the delightful name of *Cica Cica Boom*.

The entrance to the club is just a single door under a red canopy. Francesco rings the bell. A small flap in the door is lifted and two eyes stare out at us. Francesco waves a card in front of the eyes and the door is opened by a large black man. A young girl wearing an outfit that doesn't leave much to the imagination is seated at the reception desk. Francesco signs us in as his guests.

Inside the club, small alcoves lit by candlelight are furnished with low sofas and soft red velvet cushions. It takes my eyes a few minutes to adjust to the dim light. A few couples are lounging on the sofas and several couples are dancing to soft smoochy music. I think we're in a *bordello*. Francesco orders champagne and dances with us in turn.

At the end of the evening he asks for our telephone numbers, before putting us into a taxi and handing me 50,000 lire for the fare. A perfect gentleman!

Natale

Christmas is coming! The shops are full of Christmas decorations and *panettone*—a traditional sponge-like, rather dry sweetbread that comes in fancy boxes—lines the shelves.

A huge pine tree and a crib with life-size figures in St Peter's Square attract many visitors. In Piazza Navona, stalls dressed with fairy lights selling all kinds of Christmas decorations, toys and books have been erected. It looks like a fairyland.

On Christmas Day the city will shut down while everyone visits friends and relatives. It's a traditional family day.

Two weeks before Christmas, Gayle receives some sad news that her aunt in America, who has been like a mother to her, is terminally ill. Gayle makes plans to leave as soon as possible for America, not knowing if, or when, she'll be back. I'm devastated.

Frankie will spend Christmas and New Year with his 'surrogate parents', his drama teacher and her husband, at their house in Castel Gandolfo, which he has been doing for the last few years. Chris is busy singing in the choir at the Pantheon and St Peter's, and friends will be visiting him from America.

In the absence of any sort of invitation from Alessandro, I decide to go home for Christmas and New Year. I really need to bring some more teaching books and warmer clothes. I didn't realise it could get so cold in Rome.

My last teaching day is at Piazza Bologna. I will be leaving a week before the school officially closes.

When I tell my students that they will have a substitute teacher for the last week, Stefano, as spokesman, tells me that they will not take lessons that week, but will wait until I return, as they don't want anyone else to teach them. I feel flattered.

As usual, he lingers behind after class, takes my hand in his and wishes me *'Buon Viaggio.'* Oh, if only I were twenty years younger!

Gayle wants to make one last visit to Piazza Navona. So, armed with my camera, we arrive at the Piazza one chilly night. We sit outside one of the little bars near Alessandro's stand. He sees us and waves. Wearing light grey slacks and a black polo-neck sweater he looks absolutely gorgeous.

A few minutes later the waiter appears at our table with a bottle of wine and pours two glasses. '*Complimenti*' he says, nodding in the direction of Alessandro.

Before we leave the piazza we walk over to thank Alessandro for the wine. Gayle's Italian is better than mine, so she explains to him that she is leaving for America and that I will be going back to London for the holidays. She then asks him if she can take a few photos, and taking the camera from my hands, nudges me over towards him. He doesn't seem to mind, and puts his arm around me posing for the photo.

He's captured at last. At least on film. Now I'll have a photo of him to drool over.

The night before Gayle is due to leave, Frankie and I arrange a surprise farewell party for her at his place. It's a very emotional evening.

I've managed to get a flight to London that leaves around the same time as Gayle's flight to Los Angeles, so we leave for the airport together the next day.

She has many bags and, as usual, I have my camera to hand. I take a few shots of her sitting on top of all her bags. I dread to think how much she will have to pay in excess baggage. We take photographs of each other standing in front of the large Christmas tree, which is covered in shiny red baubles, and then I accidentally drop my camera on the stone floor. It damages the zoom lens. It will not operate. I feel it is symbolic.

We hug each other goodbye and Gayle promises that she will return when her aunt's affairs are in order, as she feels that she has unfinished business here. I'm sad that she's leaving Rome.

Villa Borghese

A new year, and back in Rome I head straight for Piazza Navona. Although it was good to catch up with friends again in London, I couldn't wait to get back to the Eternal City.

While I was home I managed to get my camera repaired and, fortunately, the film was not ruined as I'd feared. The photograph of Alessandro in Piazza Navona had turned out well, except that the long, skinny balloons for sale on the toy stall behind him appeared to be sitting on top of his head! Nevertheless, I carried the precious image around with me all the time. Now I've got withdrawal symptoms and need to see him in the flesh.

I decide to surprise him. I enter the Piazza from the south end, which gives me time to walk across the Piazza to where Alessandro works at the north end, so I will see him before he sees me. I am the one who is surprised. He's not there. In fact, none of the artists are there. It's too cold. Disappointed, I pull my warm jacket tighter around me and head for home.

The telephone is ringing as I open the door to my apartment. It's Franco phoning from Milan. He will be in the city on business tomorrow, and would like to invite me to lunch.

Looking very debonair, with a camel-coloured woollen coat slung around his shoulders, he's waiting for me at the appointed restaurant the following day. He wines and dines me and then takes me to his hotel in the Termini area. He's great in the sack and I really do fancy him, but he seems very cagey about what he actually does for a living. When he confides in me that he has a gambling problem and that's why his marriage broke up, warning bells start ringing in my head, so when he says he has some business to attend to, I'm relieved to leave.

Although he says he will contact me within the next few days, I think we both know that he will not.

Back to school tomorrow, but first I have an *appuntamento* in Parioli.

One of Gayle's other jobs was child minding for a family in Parioli, an exclusive residential district with imposing *palazzi,* near the Villa Borghese. Before she left Rome, Gayle recommended me to the family as her replacement for the position. I have an appointment this afternoon to meet up with the parents of the child.

Susanna and Gianni's apartment is in a tall, three-storey *palazzo* enclosed with wrought-iron gates. Their apartment is on the ground floor and they are fortunate enough to have a large garden.

Announcing myself to the *portiere,* he escorts me to the apartment. The Filipino housekeeper opens the door and shows me into a modern, elegant sitting room. French windows overlook their private garden.

I immediately like Susanna and Gianni, who both speak very good English. They particularly want an English-speaking nanny for their son, Marco, who is two. Marco will eventually go to an English school in Rome. Susanna is pregnant and is expecting the baby at the end of February. Her husband, Gianni, has his own business.

Over coffee, Susanna and I discuss hours and remuneration. I will be paid 192,000 lire per week from 8 am. until 1 pm. Monday to Friday. I meet Marco, a lovely looking boy, with thick golden hair and big brown eyes. I am only too happy to have the extra work for a few hours in the mornings, and agree to start the following week.

I head home, cook some pasta, and sit down to do my lesson plan for school this evening.

My students at the school in Piazza Bologna are all very happy to see me, especially Stefano.

I'm very attracted to him. Sometimes it feels as though we

are the only two people in the classroom. He's always the last student to leave when the lesson has finished, on the pretext of asking a question.

'*Tu sei bella,*' he whispers to me after class. He uses the familiar *tu*.

'Thank you.' I feel myself blushing, turn away quickly, and start to gather up my books from the table.

He persists. 'I don't know what is happening.'

'Stefano,' I sigh. I wish he wouldn't look at me like that. I look him straight in the eyes but feel myself getting hot and bothered. 'I'm your teacher, and old enough to be your mother,' I add.

He laughs at that, which breaks the intensity of the moment. Then his friend returns to see where he is, and off he goes.

I'd promised myself I wouldn't get involved with any of my students, but have to admit Stefano would make a lovely toy-boy!

Frankie is at EUR on Wednesday. We hug and kiss like long-lost friends and I suddenly realise how much I missed him.

On Monday morning I arrive at Susanna's apartment a few minutes before eight o'clock. Gaetano, the porter, has been told to expect me. He is quite elderly, has a kind face and twinkling blue eyes. He calls me *signorina*, a title usually reserved for younger women, so I feel quite flattered!

Susanna opens the door. She is ready to leave for work and seems relieved to see me.

'*Buongiorno,*' she greets me. Marco is still eating *prima colazione*, breakfast, but as soon as he's finished I should dress him and take him to the park for a little air. She will be home around one o'clock, she informs me. Handing me a very large key, she instructs me to turn the key three times in the door to lock it, if I go out before the housekeeper arrives. Then she kisses Marco and with a '*Ciao tesoro*' leaves. Gianni, her husband, has already left for his office.

I wait until Marco has finished his breakfast and then dress him. Susanna has left some clothes out for him to wear. Marco is a very calm boy with a sunny disposition and, considering he met me only briefly, is very well-behaved.

Around ten o'clock, the Filipino housekeeper arrives. She speaks a little English and tells me her name is Lin.

I put Marco in his pushchair and we leave for the extensive Villa Borghese gardens nearby. It's a cold, but sunny day. We walk for a few minutes and then I see a group of nannies with their charges. They all seem to know Marco. I chat with several of the girls who are nearly all Italian. It's a good way to practice my Italian, but of course as soon as they know I'm an English teacher, they want to speak English with me.

One of Marco's little friends, also called Marco, is with his babysitter, Eleanor. She speaks excellent English and we spend the morning together.

At noon, when we are ready to return home, a deep boom resounds over the park. I ask Eleanor what it is. She explains that it's the midday cannon, which is fired once daily from Gianicolo Hill in the direction of the River Tiber, to signal the exact time.

When I return to the house with Marco, a woman is in the kitchen. She introduces herself as Gianni's mother, Elena. She's prepared some lunch for Marco and also a meal for the family when they arrive home later.

After Marco has finished his lunch I attempt to put him down for a little nap in his room, as Susanna instructed, but he cries for *nonna*, who takes charge. When he's settled down Elena leaves.

Susanna arrives home from work shortly after.

'*Tutto bene?*' She is anxious to know if the morning went well.

When I assure her that Marco and I had a wonderful time, she looks very relieved.

'*A domani.*' Until tomorrow!

Every day that week Marco and I follow a similar routine. He's a cute little boy, very observant and curious about his surroundings. One morning we stroll down to the Giardino Zoologica in the park and watch the pretty pink flamingos through the fence. There is a colourful toy stall nearby. I strike up a conversation with the vendor, who tells me his name is Giancarlo. He gives Marco a small toy.

Eleanor and I have become friends, and spend a lot of time in the park with the two boys, who play happily together.

On one of our walks I discover a villa undergoing extensive renovations. Eleanor tells me that it's the Galleria Borghese art gallery, which has been closed for restoration work for several years. No-one seems to know when it will re-open.

Adjacent to the Villa Borghese is the Pincio, a beautiful garden with a panoramic terrace above the Piazza del Popolo. At weekends the Pincio is a popular family venue, with activities for children, one of them an authentic puppet theatre.

At lunchtime every day, when I arrive home with Marco from the park, Gianni's mother, Elena is in the kitchen preparing a meal for the family.

One day Elena is cooking *Carciofi alla Romana* which, she tells me, is one of Gianni's favourites. She gives me a quick cookery lesson!

Elena and Marco have a very close relationship, so naturally he always wants her to feed him and put him down for his afternoon nap. At the end of the week when I express my concerns to Susanna that Marco wants his *nonna* to do everything for him, she shakes her head and says Marco is a little *birichino*. When she sees the horrified look on my face, she smiles and tells me it's a nice way of saying 'little devil'.

The following week when I return home from the park with Marco at lunchtimes Elena is not at the house; however, delicious food is always ready and waiting on the stovetop!

Although Susanna is a capable, responsible wife and mother, she is also a career woman. Like most of her counterparts, trying to hold down a full-time job and look after a family takes its toll on her. They are modern Italians who eat out regularly. Convenience foods are not readily available in Italy. Most Italians cook with fresh produce bought from the local markets on a daily basis.

Sciopero is a word that I hear many times before I learn that it means 'strike'.

Walking Marco home from the Villa Borghese one lunchtime I hear people calling to each other, '*C'e un' sciopero.*'

Elena is at the house when I return. I ask her what *sciopero* means. She tells me that it's a transport strike and advises me to leave immediately so that I'm not stranded. For once I'm grateful that she is still at the house. I race to get the bus to Termini and the *metro* to the school in Piazza Bologna, before the whole transport system grinds to a halt.

The strike lasts only for a few hours, but long enough to cause total chaos, *che casino*! It's my first taste of what would become a regular occurrence.

There are many lightning strikes and *manifestazione*, demonstrations, in Rome. The police cordon off whole areas of the centre, which quickly disrupts the city.

One of the first *manifestazione* that I encountered shortly after my arrival in Rome was a demonstration against racism. Hundreds of people marched through the streets to the Piazza del Popolo—the aptly named Square of the People—a huge piazza at the end of the Via del Corso.

The piazza was thronging with people, many holding banners or red flags with the Communist emblem of the hammer and sickle. A noisy, nameless rock band played on a temporary stage. It was more like a celebration.

Just before elections there are many political rallies. Large red posters announcing a *manifestazione* with the sign of the hammer and sickle are posted over the city. I am surprised that the Communist Party is still active here.

Considering the Italians are such passionate people, there is very little violence at any of these large gatherings. They never seem to get out of hand. The police stand around casually in groups talking, joking, and laughing with the demonstrators.

Even when fighting for their rights, the Italians do it with style!

CARCIOFI ALLA ROMANA
(Elena's Recipe)

Ingredients:

8 small artichokes
Juice of 1 lemon
1 clove garlic, chopped
8 tablespoons olive oil
Parmesan cheese
Breadcrumbs
Salt
Pepper

Preparation:

Remove outer leaves of artichoke. Trim the tips off the leaves and the skin off the stem.

Open leaves and remove beard from centre. Place in cold water and lemon juice for 15 minutes.

Prepare breadcrumb stuffing by mixing breadcrumbs with oil, salt and grated parmesan.

Remove artichokes from water, open leaves and fill centre with breadcrumb stuffing.

Place artichokes upside down (stem up), tightly against each other in a tall pot. Add olive oil, garlic and enough water to just cover stems. Cover pot and cook on medium heat for 30–45 minutes or until tender.

Cool and place in a deep dish.

Drizzle with cooking juice.

Buono!

Amici

After Gayle's abrupt departure, I'm missing some female company, so on Sunday morning I decide to try and track down Dawn, my fellow student from the Italian class in London.

The address I have is in the Via Torino just off Via Nazionale in the Quirinale district.

I take the bus to Termini and walk down the Via Nazionale until I reach Via Torino. It's quite difficult to work out the numbering system, as shops have consecutive numbers, while the apartments above them have different consecutive numbers.

I walk up and down the street several times before I find number 41, which is a four-storey *palazzo* with a roof garden. It has an ochre-washed façade and green wooden shutters. The wooden entrance doors set in a huge stone arch are open, and a *portiere* sits in a little office just inside the cobble-stoned courtyard. I announce myself to the porter.

Although it's been more than six months since I saw her in Florence, I'm keeping my fingers crossed that she is still at this address. She is. The porter picks up the phone to let her know that '*Signora Margaret e arrivata.*' There's a pause, during which time my heart sinks. 'She's forgotten me,' I think to myself.

Next minute, I hear a muffled scream down the telephone line. The porter smiles at me and indicates the staircase. '*Prego. Quattro piano.*' It's on the fourth floor and there is no lift.

At the top of the third flight of stairs I hear a voice above me. I look up to see Dawn's face peering down at me over the staircase.

'Come on. Only one more flight,' she laughs.

I arrive at her door huffing and puffing, making a mental note to do more exercise.

'Glad you made it,' she says.

'Me too. One more flight of stairs and I probably wouldn't have.'

She giggles. 'To Rome, I mean.'

She ushers me into her apartment and I flop down in one of the big, battered leather sofas. It's all very old and shabby, but comfortable. She has the roof terrace, so we move outside with a bottle of wine and spend a couple of hours catching up with all our gossip.

Dawn is working for the United Nations Food and Agricultural Organisation, which is affectionately known in Rome as La FAO, (pronounced *la fow*). She invites me to have lunch with her at work the following day and tells me to bring my passport.

The next morning, after I leave Susanna's house, I take the bus to Termini and the *metro* to Circo Massimo. The Organisation is situated in a large grey concrete '60s style building facing the Aventino. Security is strict. My passport is kept at the desk in the lobby and in exchange I am given a security badge to wear. I then have to wait for Dawn to sign me in as a visitor, before escorting me to the restaurant.

The Casa Bar is the informal self-service cafeteria on the ground floor. For 5,000 lire I have the most divine salad, with a warm *Rosette* bread roll. We then move to the more formal restaurant on the top floor of the building for dessert and coffee.

The restaurant has a large outside terrace, from which the views are absolutely breathtaking. The Colosseum is opposite and to the right is Terme di Caracalla, the ruins of the Roman baths. Looking to the left I can see the Palatine Hill, which is one of the Seven Hills of Rome and Circo Massimo, the ancient public arena and chariot racing venue. We have *tiramisu* and a *cappuccino* on the terrace, in the watery winter sun. Tall cypress and pine trees line the Aventino and the musky smell of pines waft across to us in the breeze. What a wonderful way to dine.

I have now been in Rome for five months. I promised myself that when I got back to Rome after Christmas I would look for another apartment. I am fed up with the sloppy behaviour of my flatmates. They're a great bunch of guys, but I cannot live in these conditions. It always seems to fall on me to clean and tidy up, even though we do have a cleaning rota. So even when it's not my turn, I need to do it before I can sit and enjoy my breakfast.

Shortly after I arrived I had roped-in Ava to help me to spring-clean the kitchen. We spent a whole Saturday washing, bleaching, disinfecting, scrubbing and polishing, until everything was pristine. We could have eaten off the floor. Pots and pans hung along the wall, all bright and shiny. Everything sparkled.

Needless to say, it didn't last long, and gradually reverted to its previous chaotic state.

Now that I have two wages coming in I can start to look for somewhere else. I would prefer to share with one other person. I broach the subject of sharing an apartment with Frankie but he declines the offer.

For 1,000 lire I buy the bi-weekly magazine for expats *Wanted in Rome* and scan the pages for accommodation. I find an advert:

> Flat share—Responsible mature person m/f to share
> apartment with one American lady, in quiet suburb,
> own room/shower, 500,000 lire monthly.
> Tel. 7005968

Sounds ideal.

I telephone the number listed and a female voice answers, *'Pronto.'*

I respond in English. After exchanging a few formalities, we arrange a mutually convenient time for me to view the apartment, which is in Via Caulonia, a little further out from where I am at present. The area is not as trendy as San Giovanni, but more '*Romana*', a typical working-class neighbourhood.

I take the bus to Piazza Zama, and make the short walk to the apartment building. It's a modern apartment block in a quiet suburb. There are nine floors. The building is colour washed in sienna with green shutters. It looks well kept.

Locating the intercom on the wall I push the button for apartment number 2. The door opens with a buzz. When I step inside the vestibule area on the ground floor, a young woman with long blonde hair is waiting at the apartment door.

'Hi, come in, I'm Gabriella.' She speaks with an American accent.

I follow her along a corridor into a pleasant sitting room. French windows lead out onto a small paved courtyard, enclosed with a low stone wall and a wire fence covered in trailing vines. Large terracotta pots placed around the patio are brimming with colourful plants, and a small wrought-iron table and chairs sit under a large striped green and white parasol. It's delightful.

She offers me a soft drink, *analcolico,* and we sit together in the courtyard.

Gabriella hails from San Francisco and has been in Rome for five years, working as a freelance journalist. She has a Sicilian boyfriend and speaks perfect Italian. Her previous flatmate has already moved out, so the room is free. Gabriella rents the apartment from an Italian couple who live nearby.

When I see the accommodation available, my mind is made up. Although the bedroom is small with only a single bed, it's clean and larger than my room in Via Gallia. The bonus is that I will have my own bathroom!

'If you want the room I think we'd get on very well,' she says.

I have already made up my mind that I want it.

'I'd love it,' I reply. 'How soon can I move in?'

'How does the end of the month sound?' she asks.

It sounded perfect.

Three more weeks. I can just about survive the conditions at my present apartment until then.

'Great,' I exclaim. 'I'll be here.'

When I get back to the apartment in Via Gallia and see the usual chaos, I wonder how I've managed to stick it out for so long, but knowing I will be leaving soon makes it more bearable.

Ava looks quite crestfallen when I announce to her that I will be leaving at the end of the month and, although we don't socialise together, I think she has enjoyed the company of another woman around the house.

Now I feel more settled in Rome I decide look up my third contact, Flavia's friend, Franca.

I pluck up the courage to make the telephone call. Because of my poor Italian it would be much easier to make initial contact face-to-face, but I am reluctant to just turn up on her doorstep. I hope she speaks some English.

She answers the telephone with '*Pronto.*' It throws me completely as I expect a *'Ciao'* or a more formal *buongiorno*. For a moment all my practiced lines go out of my head. Then, falteringly, I speak.

'*Sono Margaret da Londra, amica di Flavia,*' I respond. It's also been more than six months since I met Flavia in Fiesole, and I hope she told Franca that I may be contacting her.

It seems that she did.

'*Aah! Mar-ga-ret*!' She pronounces my name with the stress equally on the three syllables.

'*Dov'e sei. A Roma?*' She sounds genuinely pleased to hear from me and immediately starts to talk to me in both Italian and English. She speaks about as much English as I do Italian, but we muddle through and she invites me over to her apartment for lunch on Sunday.

The following Sunday I stop at the flower stall at the end of Via Gallia to buy some flowers for Franca. I'm eyeing the chrysanthemums when the vendor asks me what the occasion is, explaining to me that in Italy chrysanthemums are for funerals! He also says that one should always give an odd number of flowers. I choose a bunch of mixed blooms, thanking him profusely.

I've already checked my map. I take the bus to Campo de' Fiori, walk through the Campo into Piazza Farnese and then through one of the little side streets onto the swanky Via Giulia.

At Franca's four-storey *palazzo*, I face two enormous wooden doors. On each one there is a brass lion's head with a snake-entwined ring held in its jaws. I look for the *citofono*. To my left, a small brass plate set into the wall has her name inscribed on it. I press the button next to her name.

A husky voice answers. '*Pronto.*'

'*Ciao Franca, sono Margaret.*'

'*Ciao, Mar-ga-ret. Vieni.*' As she asks me to enter, a small door set into one of the huge oak doors unlocks with a buzzing sound.

I step through the door into a cobble-stoned courtyard. At the end of the courtyard, two wrought-iron gates stand open to reveal a small garden with a central fountain. From the vaulted ceiling, two large wrought-iron chandeliers hang on iron chains. There are four doorways in the courtyard and to my right there is a short flight of red-carpeted stairs. I hesitate, wondering which one is the entrance to Franca's apartment, when I hear another buzz, and one of the doors swing open to reveal a flight of stone stairs. I climb up three flights before reaching Franca's apartment. She is already on the landing waiting for me.

'*Ciao Mar-ga-ret. Finalmente.*' She embraces and kisses me the Italian way, on both cheeks. '*Prego.*' As Franca welcomes me into her home, a small dog runs excitedly around her feet.

I enter the tiny vestibule and she ushers me into the lounge, which has high ceilings with wooden beams. The furniture is antique, the floors wooden and shiny with exotic oriental rugs scattered over them. Books completely cover one wall from floor to ceiling. A ladder on runners enables the books on the upper shelves to be reached. The lighting is subdued and the unmistakable voice of Mina, the famous Italian diva, drifts through the apartment from the CD player.

Pouring two glasses of *Chianti Classico* wine Franca gestures me to follow her.

'I am in the chicken,' she says.

I stifle a giggle. It's a common mistake with my English students to muddle chicken with kitchen. I smile and politely correct her English, whereupon she bursts into a hearty laugh. We end up laughing together. I like this woman. Sicilian born, darkly vivacious and with an infectious sense of humour, I feel that we will become good friends.

'*Salute.*' She raises her glass and I return the toast. The language barrier is not a problem. We talk non-stop, making lots of mistakes and having lots of laughs too.

Franca is a doctor of psychology. She sees patients in her home. A chaise longue sits in the corner of her lounge. I feel so comfortable in her company that I could easily lie down on it and tell her my life history!

A light breeze stirs the cream-coloured gossamer drapes at the open window. The evanescent evening light lengthens the shadows on the wall. I love this time of day, twilight. The whole ambience of the room is one of peace and tranquillity.

The little Cairn terrier is called Alice (pronounced Aleeshay). Later that evening, after an authentic Sicilian meal of *Pasta alla Norma,* we take a *passeggiata* with Alice along Via Giulia.

This picturesque cobble-stoned street, in the heart of the historic centre, and one of the oldest in Rome, extends from the church of San Giovanni dei Fiorentini to the Ponte Sisto. The Via Giulia distinguishes itself from most other streets in Rome because it is one of the only straight thoroughfares in the city and runs parallel with the River Tiber. Via Giulia boasts numerous artisan shops and magnificent *palazzi* that once housed noble Roman families. The large doorknockers on some of these buildings almost need two hands to lift them!

Hidden behind the enormous oak doors are little courtyards, some with fountains and others with frescoed walls and chandeliers. A walk along Via Giulia is a walk in ancient Rome.

One such *palazzo* has a discreet stone plate near the door that reads 'Anti-Mafia Headquarters!'

A beautiful stone arch, designed by Michelangelo and intended to be part of a bridge, spans the Via Giulia. Long tassels of green ivy cascade over the bridge towards the ground.

Franca and I continue walking through Piazza Farnese, past Palazzo Farnese, which is now the French Embassy, and through Campo de' Fiori, where there is an open-air market every morning. Franca points out a statue in the centre of the

Campo and explains that it is the statue of Giordano Bruno, a Carthusian monk burned at the stake as a heretic here in the Campo in 1606.

From the Campo we cross the Corso Vittorio Emanuele II into Piazza Navona. Alice jumps into the Fontana del Moro, and then runs towards us and proceeds to shake herself all over us, barking excitedly. I have a surreptitious look to see if Alessandro is there, but I don't see him.

Later that night as Franca and I say our farewells, I feel I have made a true friend.

I decide it's time to head for Piazza Navona again to see if Alessandro has returned. He's there, unsuspecting, sitting on a stone bench, so I creep up behind him and put my hands over his eyes. I don't say a word.

He hesitates for only a moment and then says, 'Cold fingers from London, *ciao Mar-ga-ret*.' I'm flattered that he knows it's me. But then who else would he be expecting?

He turns around, wraps me in his arms and hugs me tightly. Boy, he feels so good! At that moment it starts to rain.

'We can go to the bar,' he suggests.

I don't hesitate. 'OK,' I reply, 'I could do with a stiff one.' I smile as I say it. I know the innuendo is lost on him.

Quickly covering his paintings with a waterproof sheet, we run to the bar together. Finding a quiet corner, he orders a bottle of red wine and pours two glasses. *'Salute,'* he raises his glass to me and I raise mine to touch it. As our eyes meet, our fingers touch and I feel a jolt like an electric shock pass through my body. I wonder if he felt it too.

We sit together in comfortable silence. Our eyes do most of the talking. We wait for the rain to stop. It doesn't. It's coming down like stair-rods, with such relentless force that the raindrops appear to explode on impact with the ground, shattering like glass into a myriad of tiny fragments. I snuggle closer to Alessandro and raise my eyes to the heavens in silent prayer. 'Thank you.'

There's a lot I want to know about him. My mind is working

overtime. I wonder how old he is. It's hard for me to guess his age. He has a young looking face, but there are little crinkles around his eyes that give him a maturity. Or it could be from standing outside in all weathers. I'm sure he's younger than me by at least ten years. Is there someone special in his life? Is he married or maybe living with someone? Who was the woman with the child that he was talking to before Christmas? My Italian is improving and I feel more able to express myself, but I still can't bring myself to ask him if he's in a relationship with anyone. It doesn't seem appropriate having only known him such a short time. *Piano, piano.* Slowly, slowly.

Eventually, the rain eases off and we walk back into the piazza together.

'*Ciao.*' He leans towards me and kisses me lightly on the lips. It's so unexpected that I'm rendered speechless and, as he turns to greet a customer, I walk away in a daze with the warmth of his lips on mine.

I enjoy teaching at both schools. I know I will be seeing Frankie at EUR, and I have become very friendly with Luana, who transferred to my class.

At Piazza Bologna there is the Torrefazione. I hardly manage to pass by this shop en route to or from the school without stopping to buy something. Each purchase is painstakingly wrapped in colourful paper and tied up with ribbon.

Then, of course, there is Stefano, twenty-five, dark, intense, with a twinkle in his eye. He's the trouble-shooter in the classroom and often puts me on the spot by asking, 'Why eezit like dat?' Of course, sometimes I can't give him an answer, because there isn't one, so I just respond with the stock phrase: 'Don't try and analyse it, just learn it.'

It's St Valentine's Day. I'm teaching at Piazza Bologna this evening. I wear a red dress and high-heeled red shoes.

The lesson is based on the story of Valentine. I'm surprised how little the students know about it, considering the story originated in Italy and in Rome in particular. I ask them to translate a passage into English. I would like to share Stefano's dictionary version! (Correct version in italics).

> In the city of Rome when Claudius was Emperor, a priest called Valentine performed *(served)* in a holy temple. When war escaped *(broke-out)* in the Roman Empire, Claudius called *(summoned)* the citizens to war and the warring *(fighting)* did not cease *(went on)* for many years. The married men did not want to abandon *(leave)* their families to war, *(fight)* so Claudius, who was called Claudius the Cruel, instructed to be carried out *(ordered)* that no weddings should be made to happen *(take place)* and that engagements should come apart *(be broken off)*.
> Valentine used to marry men and women in mystery *(secrecy)* but eventually Claudius discovered what was happening and put the priest in prison, where he lost vitality *(languished)* and died. His friends buried him in the Church of St. Praxedes in Rome and he became a Saint. It was the fourteenth of February.

'Thank you Stefano. That was very informative,' I say, trying to keep a straight face. Mental note; teach phrasal verbs!

At the end of the lesson, Stefano hangs back as usual. He approaches me and makes a complimentary comment about my dress and shoes. He's holding something behind his back. With a flourish he produces a red rose.

I love my job!

On Wednesday at school in EUR, Frankie tells me that a friend of his will be arriving soon from Bermuda, to work in Rome. It's someone he's known for a number of years. He assures me that Eugene is just a friend. I'm pleased that he'll have someone else to hang out with. I know he misses Gayle too.

Chris and I meet up from time to time. He always takes me to interesting places. His apartment is in Monte Verdi Vecchio, a residential area in the hills above Trastevere.

Sometimes we have a quiet dinner at his place or walk across the street to the Lume di Sicilia, an authentic Sicilian restaurant, where we are greeted warmly by the owner, Luigi. Chris also introduces me to St. Andrew's Pub, where they serve English-style fish and chips!

Occasionally, we drive to Alexander Platz jazz club in Prati or to Bossa Nova, a popular Latin dance club on the outskirts of the city, and dance the night away.

Chris is fortunate enough to have a large roof *terrazzo* that encircles his apartment. We are standing together on the terrace one night after dinner, admiring the panoramic views, when he takes me in his arms and kisses me on the mouth.

'I've wanted to do that for a long time,' he admits.

That night I stay with Chris, and although he proves to be a very experienced lover, I cannot get Alessandro out of my head.

At the end of February, Susanna goes into hospital and has a baby girl. Her family rallies around, and her mother will be staying over with her for a few days, so I will not be needed. It couldn't be more convenient, as I need the time to organise my move.

The day before I'm due to move into the new apartment, I meet up with Gabriella who takes me to meet the landlords, Massimo and Maria, a lovely Italian couple who live nearby. It's quite common for Italian couples to keep a second apartment for their offspring. I sign the contract for six months and pay a deposit of 500,000 lire.

The following day Frankie comes over to Via Gallia to help me move my stuff. I bid *'Arrivederci'* to my flatmates and head off to Via Caulonia. Gabriella welcomes me at the door and, for the first time since coming to Rome, I feel a sense of belonging.

Over the next few days I explore the area. I find the local *alimentari*, grocery. There are no supermarkets in this area. I venture inside to have a look around. The varieties of meat that hang from the ceiling are all a mystery to me. There are so many trays of olives, cheeses and meats that I don't recognise. I have to enlist the help of Gabriella. I only eat brown bread at home and she tells me that I have to ask for *pane integrale*.

On Saturday morning I find an open-air fruit and vegetable market nearby, selling fresh produce, locally grown. Many of the vegetables are unfamiliar to me and it takes some time before I pluck up the courage to try some of the lesser-known varieties.

Around the corner on the Via Acaia I discover the Gelateria di San Crispino. The ice cream is divine! When I can't make up my mind which flavour I want I am offered samples, but I usually end up with my favourite *pistacchio* or *frutta di bosca*.

I make friends with the big black cat next door, who greets me every morning from the top of his garden wall.

Gabriella has a little motor scooter, *motorino,* and sometimes offers to give me a ride as far as Termini. She drives like a native Italian, weaving in and out of the traffic making her own traffic lane. I feel very vulnerable as we bump over the cobblestones. *Motorini* are very popular, and I consider buying one but quickly change my mind when I see how they drive here!

Often Frankie and I walk around Piazza Navona together in the evenings. If I stop to talk to Alessandro he gets impatient. He knows I've got the hots for Alessandro. As Frankie and I walk around the piazza, I can feel Alessandro watching me.

Sometimes when I'm alone, Alessandro will ask one of his fellow artists to look after his stand while we go to one of the bars in the piazza for a drink. One evening he takes me to Tre Scalini, a restaurant in the piazza, famous for their *tartufo*, a rich handmade chocolate ice-cream roll, which is absolutely to die for.

I'm very comfortable with him, but still feel that he's holding back for some reason. He's an enigma.

Do I have a sign over my head saying 'proceed with caution?' Perhaps I'm misreading the signals he's sending out? Maybe I should take a leaf out of my own book and, as I tell my students, try not to analyse things and just go with the flow. Gayle always used to tell me that I tried to analyse things too much.

When I leave the piazza I feel frustrated that my relationship with Alessandro doesn't seem to be progressing.

LA FAO SALAD

Put two tablespoons of tinned Canellini (small white kidney beans), including the juice, into a salad bowl.

Add one small chopped tomato.

Add a shake of salt.

Cover the beans and tomato with shredded lettuce.

Add sliced mozzarella, tinned tuna and a hard-boiled egg.

Add finely sliced red onions to the top of the salad.

Sprinkle paprika liberally over entire salad and then drizzle olive oil over the lot.

Serve with a warm crusty *rosette* bread roll.

FRANCA'S PASTA ALLA NORMA
(A Sicilian dish)

Ingredients:

6 medium-sized eggplants
3 cloves garlic, chopped
500 grams sun-ripened plum tomatoes, blanched, peeled and chopped
6–8 basil leaves, shredded
500 grams spaghetti
½ cup grated *pecorino Romano*, salted ricotta or parmesan cheese
Salt and pepper to taste
Extra-virgin olive oil

Preparation:

Wash, peel and slice the eggplant into half-inch slices, salt each side and let them sit in a colander for about an hour. Rinse them, pat dry and fry, a few pieces at a time in hot oil, turning them so both sides brown. Set them to drain on absorbent paper.

Sauté the garlic in oil and stir in the tomatoes. Season with salt and lots of pepper to taste. Reduce the heat to simmer for about 15–20 minutes. Just before it's ready add the shredded basil.

Cook the spaghetti until *al dente* and add the tomato sauce and eggplant. Sprinkle with cheese and serve with the remaining cheese on the side.

Buon Appetito!

Cats and Dogs

Feral cats abound in Rome, but in the Villa Borghese gardens there is a colony. No-one seems to know why and when they started to congregate there.

I accidentally stumble on their 'temple' one morning, when Marco and I are exploring a corner of the gardens that we haven't ventured into previously. I say temple, because the area is a small clearing that could have been an amphitheatre or place of worship, centuries ago.

Large tomb-like stones are set in a semi-circle in front of a white marble edifice, which backs onto the dividing wall between the gardens and the zoo. Stone benches, alcoves and niches, just the right size for a cat to shelter, are carved into the marble.

Considering the cats are wild, they look fairly well fed and healthy. They bask in the morning sun, stretched out on the ancient stones that are scattered around the area. Some of them are mothers with kittens.

We put cats' corner on our morning itinerary, and visit regularly.

Every morning around eleven o'clock, rain or shine, a lady in a chauffeur-driven car pulls into the park, and stops near the cat colony. The chauffeur opens the boot of the car which is full of cat food, whereupon the lady distributes the food to the cats. I guess word must have got around between those felines and that's why they congregate at that particular spot. The Good Samaritan even makes sure that they are all healthy and apparently, according to the locals, pays a veterinary surgeon to accompany her to the site. If one pussy shows signs of sickness it's whisked off to the vets!

The saying goes that there are seven rats to every cat in Rome, and if it wasn't for these feline creatures stalking around the place, it would be over-run with rodents.

While cats roam around Rome (forgive the pun) unchecked, dogs on the other hand are doted on, and are rarely seen without their owner.

Doggies and their proud owners make the *passeggiata* together. There are fines for not cleaning up doggie poo, but along with other rules and regulations are not often heeded. I have to commend Franca as she always clears up Alice's poo.

Franca invites me to Church with her one Sunday morning. She brings along Alice.

The beautiful Baroque church, San Giovanni dei Fiorentini, situated at the end of Via Giulia, is holding a *Festa di Cane*. It's the only church in Rome where animals are welcome, although in January a Blessing of the Animals takes place on the steps of Sant' Eusebio church in Piazza Vittorio.

I can't believe my eyes when I arrive at the church. I've never seen so many dogs together in one spot, except at Crufts, Britain's most prestigious dog show! They throng the steps of the church. There are all types, from the largest Great Dane to the smallest Chihuahua.

Most of the animals are well-behaved in the church and Alice sits quietly beside us throughout the service. Occasionally a dog will bark or whine, whereupon it is swiftly removed from the church, like a naughty child. At the end of the service, the owners of these canine worshipers walk or carry their dogs down the aisle, whereupon the Priest duly blesses them with a sprinkling of holy water. No, not the owners, the dogs. Unbelievable!

Franca regularly invites me to her house for lunch, which she cooks from scratch. Her cupboards and refrigerator seem devoid of food, but she always manages to produce a delicious feast made with a few fresh ingredients. The Romans have an expression—*l'arte d'arrangiarsi*—the art of adapting to one's circumstances, or the ability of making something from nothing.

One evening in March, on my way to Franca's *palazzo*, I see lots of young girls and women carrying sprigs of mimosa.

Franca explains that it's *La Festa della Donna,* or Ladies Day, when women and girls all over Italy exchange and receive bouquets of delicate yellow mimosa, as a gesture of solidarity among women. In the evening, it's traditional for groups of women to have a night out without the men.

Later that night the streets are strewn with discarded sprigs of the fragile wilted flower.

I can't help feeling sorry for these Italian women who are only allowed out with their girlfriends one night a year. At home, young women, whether married or not, often have Friday night out with the girls, as the men have Friday night out with the boys.

Although I have been told that on the surface it would appear that these Italian macho men rule the roost it is, in fact, the other way around. Here the *donna* rules. They just let the men think *they* do!

Oscar Night

Frankie's friend, Eugene, has arrived. What a flamboyant character! There is no mistaking his sexual preferences. He's tall, dark haired, and good looking (aren't they all) and very gregarious, with a dry sense of humour.

One day Eugene and I decide to explore the city. We take the *metro* and head for Piazza di Spagna.

Spring in Rome is an explosion of colour. The blossom is on the trees and the Spanish Steps are lined with large terracotta pots, overspilling with pink azaleas.

Before we climb the steps to the Church of Trinita dei Monti, we stop for a while on the elegant Via dei Condotti at the famous coffee shop, Antico Café Greco. The waiters, *cameriere*, move between the tables looking like penguins in their white shirts and black tie and tails. Some of them look as if they should have retired eons ago, but I have noticed that many waiters here in Rome are elderly, and take great pride in their work.

We watch the parade of 'fashionistas', mainly Japanese women, who are enjoying a very strong yen and snapping up goods from the designer shops. None of these women look larger than a size two or older than sixteen. They are loaded with expensive looking carrier bags from Prada, Gucci, Armani and the like. Eugene has some tongue in cheek comments to make as usual.

'Daahling, don't they look just like stick insects!'

The Trinita dei Monti sits high above the Spanish steps but is well worth the climb. From the top of the steps we look back down along the Via dei Condotti. The street is full of people as far as the eye can see. Like an army of ants. *Piena di formiche!*

An old lady sits outside the entrance to the church, her basket full of colourful scarves for visitors to cover their upper arms and shoulders, in case they have no sleeves. A great idea!

The Church of St Peter's in the Vatican City should do likewise. They have guards on 'bare shoulder duty'. Woe-betide if you have too much flesh exposed. Bare shoulders and legs will not be tolerated here. Many times I have seen tourists turned away from the church because they could not follow the strict dress code, which is shown on a notice board at the entrance to the church. They too, could have an old lady sitting at the entrance of the church with a basket full of scarves to cover bare shoulders.

Walking along the Viale della Trinita dei Monti towards the Pincio Hill, we pass the Villa Medici, which houses the Accademia di Francia. There is an exhibition of the works of Tamara di Lempicka entitled *Tra eleganza e trasgressione*. Eugene and I are both art lovers, so we buy tickets and enter the villa. I love the erotic Art-Deco style of the Polish-born artist. I buy a poster of her famous self-portrait, sitting in a green Bugatti, for my bedroom wall. Eugene and I spend a couple of hours at the exhibition.

Further along the Viale we stop at a restaurant for lunch. We choose a table on the vine-covered terrace that overlooks red-tiled rooftops, and order a glass of crisp white wine and a fresh green salad. Sheer bliss!

We are fascinated by the small turtles that are swimming around in the lily pond, situated in the centre of the terrace. They keep us amused all through lunch.

It's a beautiful day and the silence is broken only by the hypnotic trickling of the water fountain. It's so peaceful, so *tranquillo*. We are reluctant to leave. We could laze away the whole afternoon and stroll up to the Pincio as the sun goes down, but we have been invited over to Frankie's for an 'Oscar Night supper'.

We take the *metro* to Piramide and stop at the pasticceria near Frankie's house to buy dainty little bite-size cakes, which are carefully placed in a box and wrapped in fancy paper. For dinner

Frankie has made his favourite pasta dish *Penne all' Arrabbiata,* which means 'angry pasta', and a wonderfully light *tiramisu,* which translated into English means 'pick me up'.

After dinner we settle down for a 'night at the Oscars'. It's the 66th Academy Awards and Whoopi Goldberg is hosting. She is the first African American woman to host the Awards solo.

Schindler's List wins seven Oscars, and is voted Best Picture.

I was rooting for Daniel Day Lewis who was nominated as Best Actor for *In the Name of the Father,* but the Oscar went, deservedly, to Tom Hanks for *Philadelphia.*

The movie industry is alive and well in Rome, just. Actually, it's going through a bit of a slump at the moment.

Cinecitta film studios are the largest in Europe. The entrance to the studios, a stark pink building, typical of the style of Mussolini who founded the studios in 1937, is situated on the Via Tuscolana.

Many classic films have been produced there; including *Roman Holiday, Three Coins in the Fountain* and *La Dolce Vita,* and many famous actors have worked at the studios, including Sophia Loren, Gina Lollobrigida, and Claudia Cardinale, three of my favourite actresses.

The studios have also been used for many important international productions, and nearly all Federico Fellini's films were made there. His recent death is a huge loss to the movie industry.

Before Gayle left Rome she worked at the studios on the film-set of *Cliffhanger,* an action thriller starring Sylvester Stallone.

Today Cinecitta is the television industry as much as the film industry. Italian talk shows and Real TV productions are broadcast live from the studios.

It seems compulsory that television quiz shows have two *valette*; voluptuous, perfectly groomed, glamorous hostesses, usually one brunette and one blonde who say nothing, but stand either side of the host with fixed smiles on their immaculately made up faces.

So far I've spotted only one actor here in Rome. I am walking along Via Torino towards Via Nazionale one evening. I'd been to check out the Opera House, Teatro dell'Opera. It has a rather disappointing façade and an uninteresting programme. I've been thoroughly spoilt living in London with so many venues on my doorstep. However, during the summer months in Rome, performances are held in the open air at Terme di Caracalla, which are quite spectacular against the stupendous backdrop of the ruins.

Anyway, I'm walking along Via Torino. It's dark, and I hurry along to reach Dawn's apartment. There's no-one around. Then I see a man approaching me, tall, broad shouldered. I'm not afraid. Part of the joy of living in Rome is that compared to other major cities it is fairly safe, and I never feel threatened while walking along the streets at night alone, no matter how late it is.

As the man and I pass each other, I try not to make eye contact with him, but out of the corner of my eye, in that brief second before he passes me, I realise that it's Liam Neeson, the actor. I stop in my tracks and turn around, but by now he is some meters away. I resist the urge to call after him, 'Is that you Liam?'

I wondered why he was walking along the Via Torino, where he'd been and why he wasn't in a chauffeur-driven car, but I guess if you are famous, and can have some anonymity in a city, you'd probably take advantage of that and enjoy a stroll. And Rome is certainly a walking city.

Often I get up at the crack of dawn on a Sunday morning and head for Porta Portuese, the large, open air flea market in Trastevere that sells everything from antiquities, to livestock and clothing.

Gayle introduced me to Porta Portuese and her wardrobe was full of bargains from the market.

I wander among the stalls and sort through the mountains of clothes that are piled sky-high on tables. There are always lots of women picking over the clothes. Sometimes I spy something interesting and try to pull it out of the pile, only to find that some feisty Italian woman has already got her hands on it. It results in a tug of war. My opponent usually wins, my well-mannered English psyche taking over and conceding defeat.

Other tables have heaps of handbags. A lot of the stuff is second-hand and I wonder where it's all from. Frankie says they are bags that have been snatched from their owners and have been transported from Naples in lorries.

So I guess you can say it's 'off the back of a lorry'!

The market itself, and the buses to and from the market, are always packed and pickpockets are rife. The number 64 bus, which runs from Termini Station to St Peters in the Vatican City and passes through Trastevere is particularly notorious for pickpockets. Always busy, it rivals the London underground in the rush hour when everyone is jammed in like sardines in a tin and it's impossible to move a muscle.

Thieves operate in pairs and while one pushes and jostles and distracts your attention, the other is dipping his fingers into your bag. The buses have three doors, the front and rear to get on and the middle doors to get off. Sometimes in a crowded bus the two thieves split up, one working at the front end of the bus and one at the rear. If one of them has been successful, he will signal to his partner and they both get off the bus at the next stop, one from the rear door and one from the front door.

Returning from a rewarding morning at the market one Sunday, I congratulate myself on another trip to Porta Portuese without being pick-pocketed. Too soon! My wallet is stolen from my handbag during the journey on the number 64 bus back to Termini.

Fortunately, I was not carrying credit cards or very much cash, having already spent most of it. I only discovered my wallet was missing when I decided to get off the bus and use the *metro* because the traffic was gridlocked. My *tessera*, the monthly transport ticket, had also been in my wallet.

When I first arrived in Rome, I quickly learned not to stop on the street to read a map. I would check my route before I left home or go into a bar for a coffee while I studied the map. I tried not to look like a tourist and dressed so as to blend in with the locals, my camera tucked well out of sight.

In the centre of Rome there are groups of *zingari*, gypsy children. They congregate around you on the street, pushing and shoving and begging for money. A couple of them will attract your attention, while another picks your wallet.

Another ploy is to throw water or some other substance over you as if by accident, and then fuss around trying to wipe it off, while other little hands go to work. They are known to the police who, unfortunately, can do nothing about it as the children are all underage.

PENNE ALL'ARRABBIATA
(Frankie's favourite)

Ingredients:

400 grams penne pasta
120 grams pancetta or lean bacon
400 grams tomatoes
Half a chilli
1 clove garlic
5 leaves basil
80 grams butter
40 grams grated *pecorino* cheese
Salt

Preparation:

Chop the pancetta or bacon. Seed and chop the chillies. Heat the butter and add the pancetta, chilli and garlic. Cook for 8 minutes over a medium heat. Add the chopped tomatoes and season with salt and pepper. Cover and simmer for about 40 minutes.

Cook the penne until it is *al dente*.

Add the basil to the sauce. Pour the sauce over the penne and toss the two together.

Serve immediately with freshly grated *pecorino* cheese sprinkled over the top.

Stupendo!

Halcyon Days

Frankie, Eugene and I take a few trips out of Rome together. Sometimes I have to mediate as they act like a couple of melodramatic divas, although they have me in stitches.

At *Pasqua*, Easter, we visit Castel Gandolfo, a pretty hilltop town above Lake Albano in Castelli Romani, about twenty kilometres from Rome where the Pope has his summer residence.

Frankie has borrowed a car. We leave Rome along the Appian Way, the first road from Rome to Naples and the Port of Brindisi. The catacombs pass under this road, miles and miles of tunnels where early Christians buried their dead. If you like that sort of thing, it's possible to explore the labyrinthine passages by candlelight.

The first part of the Appian Way, Via Appia Antica, is paved with ancient Roman cobblestones and lined with funeral tombs. Eventually, the old road joins Via Appia Nuova, the newer part of the Appian Way, and a few kilometres later we turn off towards Castel Gandolfo.

Frankie's friends have an old red-brick farmhouse, perched on the hillside above the Lake. Jill—an American lady who came to Rome twenty years ago to teach drama for two years, met Luigi, married him and stayed—makes us very welcome. I admire the way she switches so easily between English and Italian.

From the *terrazzo* under the vine covered pergola we have a perfect view of the Papal Palace, the Pope's summer residence, on the opposite side of the lake. We drink iced tea and listen to the drone of a light aircraft that is circling the lake. It's a lazy afternoon. Later on, other friends arrive and we are invited to stay for a barbeque.

That evening we take an alternative route back to Rome, through Rocca di Papa, and Grottaferrata, two more picturesque medieval villages. We're too exhausted to explore them, so we put them on our agenda for another trip.

The first of May is a holiday. The three of us decide to hire a car and explore Nemi, in the Castelli Romani, where every May there is a *Sagra delle Fragola*, a strawberry festival. The *fragoline di bosco* are small strawberries that grow wild in the woods.

We drive along the hairpin bends of the narrow streets until we come across Sirena del Lago, a small rustic family run *trattoria* that looks inviting. We decide to stop and eat lunch here. Eugene and I choose the ravioli stuffed with truffles. It's sheer ambrosia. We both think we've died and gone to heaven!

Although we are a little early for the actual festival, the strawberries are already being harvested and we eat some of the succulent sweet berries with ice cream, for dessert.

The beautifully secluded Lake Nemi, sits in an oval-shaped volcanic crater. It's known as Diana's looking-glass because of the stillness of the water. Diana was the Goddess of the Hunt and later became known as the Moon Goddess. Every year during the August full moon, the ancient Festival of Torches is celebrated. Pilgrims carry torches and candles in a procession of twinkling lights along the Via Diana and line up by the dark waters of the lake to pay homage to the Goddess. From the vantage point on the banks where the Temple of Diana once stood, the full moon is reflected in the smooth, dark mirror of the water.

The Isle of Capri is one of my favourite spots. Frankie, Eugene and I decide to spend a weekend on the island later in May, to celebrate Frankie's birthday.

On the Saturday morning of what promises to be a blisteringly hot weekend, we meet up at Termini Station to take the train to Naples, Frankie's hometown and home to the pizza and the Mafia.

There are only two ticket windows open and the queue is

unbelievably long. We only just manage to buy our tickets with a few minutes to spare before the train departs. It's packed, but we find three empty seats in the same compartment and settle down for the two-hour journey.

Napoli! Chaotic, dirty and with an atmosphere like nowhere else I know. I'm fascinated, but at the same time feel a little vulnerable. A huge street market outside the station sells all sorts of cheap leather goods. Everyone looks dark and gypsy-looking. Vespa scooters carrying three or four people swerve around us as we try to cross the busy roads. Girls ride side-saddle, dressed in tight jeans and stiletto heels, hanging on to their boyfriends, with no helmets!

'Don't you just *love* it,' enthuses Frankie.

We book into a small hotel near the station before being picked-up by Tony, an old friend of Frankie's, who drives us to Lake Averno, a volcanic lake north-west of Naples. While eating lunch at a pizzeria overlooking the lake, Tony explains to me that the Romans regarded the lake as the entrance to the Underworld because of its gloomy aspect and sulphuric vapours.

Later that evening we stroll along the sea front. The bay of Naples sweeps around in a semi-circle and with its twinkling lights it looks very picturesque. However, the following morning, when we take the ferry over to Capri, we can see how sleazy the bay really looks

'See Naples and die,' goes the old adage. I can't wait to get to Capri!

Arriving in Capri is an unforgettable sight of blue, white and green. Beneath an azure sky, little white yachts bob up and down in the harbour. Nestling on the lush green hillside are several stupendous white villas. It's a haven for writers, artists and film stars, such as Sophia Loren and Liz Taylor.

After disembarking at the port in Capri, we take the funicular railway, which slides through dense lemon groves, up to Capri town. Below us the sea is the colour of lapis lazuli.

Ana Capri lies on a plateau above Capri town. It's very quaint, with a tangle of narrow streets snaking between whitewashed façades. In order to reach Ana Capri we must take a bus or walk. We decide to walk. It's further than we think and the sun beats mercilessly down on us.

Arriving exhausted at Ana Capri, we fall into the first bar we can find, and sit under the shade of a walnut tree. I can almost hear Sinatra crooning, 'twas on the Isle of Capri that I found her'.

We order cold drinks, relax and dream about how lovely it would be to own a villa here, when I clock a rather handsome guy at the next table eyeballing us. I realise that his interest is directed at Eugene.

'I think it's you he's interested in Eugene,' I hiss.

'Oh, I know,' responds Eugene with a salacious smile. 'Don't worry daahling, we've already made eye contact.'

Frankie just raises his eyes to the beautiful blue heaven!

A few minutes later, Mr Tall, Dark and Handsome disappears into the bar and a minute or so later, Eugene excuses himself and sashays into the bar.

'She's such a slut,' comments Frankie.

It amuses me that Frankie and Eugene often refer to each other as 'she'.

A few minutes later Eugene reappears from the bar waving a piece of paper at us.

'I got his phone number,' he says.

Judging by the grin on his face that's not all he got!

Shortly after we arrive back from Capri, my flatmate Gabriella announces that she has decided to go and live in Sicily with her boyfriend. If I want to stay on in the apartment, I will have to negotiate with Massimo the landlord and find another flatmate. I ask Eugene if he's interested.

'Daahling, that would be fabulous.'

I speak to Massimo, who invites us along to his apartment one evening. After he meets Eugene, he agrees that he can move in on the first of June. I take over the lease from Gabriella.

I thought I wouldn't see much of Frankie once Eugene

arrived, but now that Eugene and I are sharing an apartment, Frankie is always coming over to see us. When we go out we are all girls together.

They frequent L'Alibi, a gay club. Sometimes they invite me along, but I never accept. I don't think I would want to see them in action!

Behind the Vittorio Emanuele Monument in the Teatro Marcello District, is the park of Monte Caprini.

I walked into the park one day before I knew of its reputation. I strolled along little narrow pathways dotted with benches here and there, almost hidden in the bushes; discreet little arbours of love. Lots of couples sat together in these secluded spots or strolled together hand in hand. Nothing odd about that, except that they were all men! I realised that I had entered a gay cruising park!

Although the gay community is quite active in Rome, most of the venues are still under wraps, and many homosexuals are still 'in the closet'. After all, Italy is a Catholic country and the Vatican is the home of the Holy See, the central government of the Catholic Church, headed by the Bishop of Rome, the Pope!

In June, Rome holds its first Gay Pride march. Approximately 10,000 people take part. It seems that the whole gay population of Rome has come out of the closet! Eugene is, of course, among them!

The Baptism

I have been invited to the baptism of Susanna's baby. It will be held in St Peter's in the Vatican City. An Archbishop will perform the ceremony. I am flattered to be invited and readily accept the invitation—after all it's not every day the opportunity to attend a baptism in the Vatican occurs.

I ask Susanna how they managed to get such a prestigious location for the baptism. It seems that Elena's family were tailors to the clergy and the Archbishop is a friend. So it's a case of 'who you know'.

The morning of the baptism dawns clear and bright. I have arranged to go to Susanna's house early to look after Marco. I will leave from the house to the Vatican with Marco and Elena.

The house is all hustle and bustle, with people everywhere. Susanna's parents and Gianni's mother have already arrived at the house.

A party will be held in the garden after the ceremony and the caterers are at the house organising everything. The garden looks really pretty, set out with little round tables covered with starched white and pink cotton tablecloths, napkins and pink flower arrangements. Little tulle-wrapped parcels which contain five sugared almonds for each guest, sit on the tables. They are *confetti bonbonieri* and are traditional party gifts. Pink and white parasols shade each table.

It's a beautiful warm June day. I dress Marco in a little blue cotton suit. He looks so cute. Susanna and Gianni are taking their car to be valeted, so off they go. Elena and I are instructed to take a taxi to St Peter's Basilica when we are ready. Susanna's parents have dressed the baby and are ready to leave for the church in their car. The baby is with the Filipino housekeeper until Susanna and Gianni return for her.

The taxi drops Elena, Marco and I near the Vatican. Walking between the colonnades that surround the piazza, we cross the square and enter the cavernous interior of St Peter's Basilica. Although I've been inside these hallowed walls a number of times now, the sheer size of it always takes my breath away. Still, it's not one of my favourite churches as I find it too ostentatious for my taste.

As usual, there is a line of people filing past the large bronze statue of St Peter. His right foot is partly worn away by the countless pilgrims who kiss and touch it while praying for a miracle. A cluster of people are gathered around a small chapel nearby that houses the famous sculpture of Michelangelo's *Pieta*.

We notice a group of people to the left of the aisle gathered at one of the other little chapels. It's the baptism party. Everyone is now present, except for Susanna and Gianni. The Archbishop who will conduct the baptism arrives dressed in red, white and gold robes, and greets the family members.

Several minutes pass, during which everyone is making polite conversation. There is no sign of Susanna and Gianni. Then, finally, they come rushing in. After hurried salutations, hugs and kisses, Susanna smilingly looks around and asks '*Qui ha la bambina?*' Who has the baby?

There is a stunned silence in the little congregation; then her mother, surprised, exclaims, '*Pensavamo che la stavate portanda!*' We thought you were bringing her!

'*Madonna!*' We all realise that no-one has brought the baby, she is still at home!

After some frantic discussion, the Archbishop agrees to hold up the baptism ceremony for as long as he can, as he has another one scheduled in half an hour, while Gianni races back home to get the precious little bundle.

The minutes tick by. Marco is getting bored and fidgety. He's discovered the pockets in his suit and is fiddling around with them. Boring of that game, he sits down on the floor. A hush has fallen over the small congregation. Everyone, including the Archbishop, is trying not to appear anxious. I discreetly look at my watch. The normal journey time from St Peter's to Parioli and back would be about thirty-five minutes. I'm praying for a miracle.

Gianni is an extremely fast driver and has a BMW. He's back at the Basilica, clutching the baby, with about ten minutes to spare. Finally, the ceremony proceeds. Gianni lights a long tapering candle which he, Susanna, the godparents and the Archbishop all hold together, while the blessing is read. The Archbishop then sprinkles the baby's head with holy water and Monica Valeria is baptised.

I look towards the bronze statue of St Peter facing us on the opposite side of the church and bow my head in silent thanks. '*Grazie, San Pietro per il miracolo!*'

Back at the house we have afternoon tea in the garden. We're all relieved that what could have been a major catastrophe had been averted!

Later, I take the opportunity of speaking to the Filipino maid who was literally left 'holding the baby'. She didn't seem to think it very strange that everyone had gone off to a baptism without the baby, and thought maybe that's the way they do it in Italy!

My journey to Susanna's house in Parioli takes me through Termini Station. The traffic is always gridlocked, which allows me ample time to observe the characters that hang around the rather seedy area near the station.

One morning on the Via Gioberti, just before the bus turns into Termini, I notice a woman standing in a doorway, lighting up a cigarette. Her stance is provocative and her clothes are tarty looking. She wears a skirt that is little more than a curtain pelmet. With bright red hair, obviously out of a bottle, and garish make-up, her appearance leaves nothing to the imagination as to her profession. She is *una puttana*—a prostitute—and she's no spring chicken either.

She intrigues me and I start to look out for her every morning.

On some occasions I see her talking to a man, probably negotiating a price. When I don't see her in her usual spot, I guess that she is already at work with a customer, doing business.

I start wondering about her and how many customers she could 'service' in one day. I wonder how much she charges, think of a number, and do some calculations:

If she charges, say, 40,000 lire—about 20 pounds—for a session, and has eight customers a day, that would be 160 pounds. If she works five days, that's 800 pounds! It's quite mind-boggling to think that she could be earning a lot more money than me. I'm definitely in the wrong job.

I nickname her Mary, although she is definitely no virgin.

Then one day she isn't in her usual spot and I never see her again. I like to think that she met someone who took her away from it all, like Richard Gere did with Julia Roberts in the movie *Pretty Woman*; but in reality there was probably a much more sinister reason for her disappearance.

On Via Appia there are lots of girls, some local, but mostly from Eastern European countries, who line the road waiting for kerb-crawlers anxious to procure a 'lady of the night'. Sometimes these girls mysteriously disappear and are never found. It's a risk of the profession. I wonder if Mary finished up there.

On the crowded bus to Susanna's house one morning, I have managed to get a seat. A middle-aged man in a business suit is standing in the aisle near me.

As each person passes behind him in order to get off the bus, he pushes himself against me. His crotch is level with my shoulder. At first I ignore it, giving him the benefit of the doubt that it's by accident, but as the bus empties out and there are seats available, he doesn't move. Now he is pressing himself against my shoulder and swaying with the motion of the bus.

When we go round a corner he presses himself really hard against me.

Not being the shy and retiring English lady I used to be when I first arrived, I turn around in my seat to face him, make eye contact and hiss '*Stronzo*', which means pig or turd! I prefer the latter. I haven't got the courage or the language to rant and rave and make a scene, but that one word and the look obviously did the trick, because he moved away from me real sharpish, and got off at the next bus stop.

Troppo Caldo!

Summer is upon us and school's out. Although I still manage to get to Piazza Navona, Alessandro is usually only there from late afternoon, and works well past midnight because the weather is so hot. I usually just stop to say hello, sometimes have a quick drink with him and head home. He tells me that he will be away for the month of August visiting family in Milan. Piazza Navona just won't be the same without him.

1994 is a long hot summer. In July, Franca invites me to go to the Amalfi Coast with her. She brings Alice, her little dog.

We drive out of Rome, arriving in Amalfi in the early evening. We haven't made a room reservation, so we drive along the beautiful winding coastal road, which is cut into the side of a mountain, stopping here and there at small hotels in search of a room.

Eventually, we find a small boutique hotel in Positano, which has only one room available. It's ideal. It has a balcony from which we can see the whole coastline, stretching up to Ravello.

One evening, we meet up with some friends of Franca's who are also holidaying on the coast. We join them for drinks at a bar on the beach.

The 1994 FIFA World Cup is being televised on a big screen. The bar is jam-packed with football supporters and the game dominates the conversation. It's the final and Italy is playing Brazil. Football leaves me cold. I have no interest in the game, but it's an infectious atmosphere and I get caught up in the excitement and start to enjoy it, cheering or groaning along with the locals at the appropriate moments. The game ends with a 0–0 score after extra time.

It's a penalty shoot-out. The bar is as silent as the grave. Brazil scores three penalty goals. Italy scores two, with one more shot to go. Now everybody in the bar is on their feet including me. It all rests on the shoulders of Roberto Baggio. Everyone holds their breath. He shoots—and the ball sails over the bar. Baggio stands in front of the goal, arms at his side in disbelief.

Brazil has won 3–2 in a penalty shoot-out. The small contingent of Brazilians in the town, celebrate their victory. A short cavalcade of cars drive through the streets, their horns beeping, with the green, yellow and blue Brazilian flag flying from the windows. And all around me in the bar, grown men weep like children!

Franca and I stay in Positano for ten days. On the last day, we are walking back to our hotel from the beach along a steep path, when Alice stops and sits down. Franca calls her several times, but she won't budge. Finally, Franca has to pick her up and carry her. Alice doesn't seem her usual playful self. Franca is concerned about her, so when we get back to Rome she takes her to the Vet. Alice has a heart problem. Two weeks after we return from our holiday, Alice dies. Franca is inconsolable.

It's hot in Rome. We've had no rain for almost two weeks. Frankie and I decide to go to the beach for the day.

I take the *metro* to Piramide and meet Frankie at Ostia Railway Station, where the train departs for Ostia Lido, a seaside resort, twenty-three kilometres south-west of Rome. The train is crowded with Italian families, all with the same idea of trying to escape the heat of the city. There is no air-conditioning on the train.

After half an hour we arrive at Ostia. We're grateful for the *ponentino*, the sea breeze that rises in the early afternoon, which is drifting into the open window of the train.

We join the crowd of people heading for the beach, manage to find a relatively private spot on the black sand, and settle down for the afternoon. I have a surreptitious look around at the talent on the beach. Considering this is a Catholic country, some of the bikinis are really skimpy and hardly cover the essentials. All the young women have fabulous figures and the men are all bronzed with rippling muscles. They also wear the skimpiest of swimming trunks, which don't leave much to the imagination. The men really love to strut their stuff. In my shorts and top I feel overdressed. Frankie has on some colourful flowery shorts. We stick out like sore thumbs!

Ferragosto comes in the middle of August. It is one of the most observed Italian public holidays, and practically all of Italy comes to a halt. Most Italians take their annual holiday during this month, the hottest of the year. They pile into their cars and leave the towns to the elderly and the tourists, or the unfortunate few who have to work. They, like us, will not join in the mass exodus from the steaming hot city to another house in the country, the mountains, or by the sea.

Fregene is a sun-swept town on the Tyrrhenian coast about thirty-eight kilometres west of Rome. More upmarket than the congested beaches of Ostia Lido, the beaches at Fregene are mainly owned by privately run clubs or *Stabilimenti Baleari.*
Fregene had its heyday in the '60s and '70s, when it was the 'in' place to be. It was frequented by the likes of Federico Fellini, the film director, and Marcello Mastroianni, the actor. It became an oasis for intellectuals and Rome's fashionable crowd.
Franca is a member of one of the clubs and goes regularly. She loves the beach and is very *abbronzata*—tanned. I'm lily-white compared to her.
 One Sunday she invites me to join her. I'm not really one for lying on a beach frying myself to a burnt crisp, but as it's now September and a little cooler, I agree to go with her. It will be good to escape the hustle and bustle of the city.
We find a parking spot along the beach road, and after paying the attendant, cross the road into the club. The sands are golden and very clean and I'm happy to see that it's not too busy.
A few brightly-striped umbrellas and sun-beds are dotted around the beach. Franca and I head to the water's edge. We

lather ourselves in sunscreen and settle down on the sands under an umbrella.

All the beautiful people of Rome are here. Lithe, tanned bodies, shiny with oil, are posing around the beach. Many of the women are topless. A few people walk along the water's edge, stopping every now and then to engage in conversation with someone. Most people seem to know each other.

As the day wears on Franca follows the sun, edging further and further away from the shade of the umbrella. I edge further and further into the shade.

A little poem by Ogden Nash keeps running through my head as I stare out to sea:

> 'How pleasant to sit on the beach,
> On the beach, on the sand, in the sun,
> With ocean galore within reach,
> And nothing at all to be done'

Later, we walk up to the restaurant on the beach and have a succulent seafood salad before heading back to Rome.

Arriving home I am glowing—literally—and look like a lobster. Why do I even bother?

Today is Marco's first day at nursery school. Susanna has asked me to arrive early so that we can take him to school together. Susanna and Gianni have chosen to send Marco to an English School, where he will learn English. They will speak to him in Italian at home. I think it's a great idea.

CORE International is a small English school near Parioli. The children are a mix of nationalities, cultures and religion. Children can attend nursery from age three to five, and then primary school until eleven, when they move on to other schools.

When I arrive at the house Marco is ready for school with his little backpack. Not quite three, he looks too small to be going to school.

Susanna drives over to the school and we take Marco inside. Marco is quite overwhelmed. After a while, Susanna hugs and kisses Marco and tells him we have to leave. He gets very upset and starts to cry. Susanna becomes very emotional and wants to stay with him a while longer, but I advise her that we should not make a fuss and just go. She takes my advice and we leave, although I know it's heart-wrenching for her to do that.

The same thing happens the following day but we leave quickly, before the situation becomes too traumatic. On the third day there are no tears as Marco has made a little friend, and he's fine. He hardly gives us a glance when we leave.

Now my routine is different. I take Marco to school on the bus, and Elena collects him in the car when school finishes at lunchtime. While he's at school, I help Susanna, who is on maternity leave, to look after Monica until Elena arrives back at the house with Marco. Susanna is due to return to work next month, so I will look after Monica.

If I want to stay in Rome and have a slice of *la dolce vita*, I need to find a rich Count—or more teaching work—Counts are a bit thin on the ground.

I advertise to tutor privately during the afternoons. I'm overwhelmed by the amount of responses I receive.

I take on three students. They each have two hours of tuition per week, which takes up three afternoons. I charge 30,000 lire per lesson, which is about 15 pounds.

Marra is fifteen and still at school. She lives in Parioli, not far from Susanna's house, so it's convenient to go straight there after babysitting. She lives in her grandmother's apartment above her parents' apartment. I never understand why.

Paolo is fourteen and also lives in Parioli. He has a good command of English, and wants to converse about current affairs and to read literature. His mother is very elegant and always looks as if she's about to leave for the theatre when I arrive, but she is a stay-at-home housewife, *casalinga*. Perhaps this is how the Italian woman keeps her husband—by looking like a million dollars while serving up the pasta!

Sergianni already has a good working knowledge of English. At thirty-something, he still lives with his parents, whom I never meet, in Prati. His father is a diplomat, and I conduct the lesson with Sergianni in his father's study. Their *palazzo* is humungous.

On one occasion, when I need to use the bathroom, Sergianni escorts me along endless, highly polished tiled floors, and waits outside the bathroom to escort me back to the study. If he didn't, I probably would have got lost. I try to pee quietly as I know he's just outside the door!

His mother is an actress, apparently quite famous, and is always resting in her bedroom while I am teaching. The house is in complete darkness, the windows and shutters closed. On several occasions while I am teaching, I hear a bell tinkling in the distance. Sergianni excuses himself, explaining that his mother needs something. I'm aghast that his mother summons him like a servant.

The relationship between mother and son in Italy seems to be something special that I haven't noticed in any other country. I have been warned that if you marry an Italian man you are also marrying his mother! *Mamma* is always on hand to do things for her son, whatever his age and marital status.

From my private tutoring, I go straight to my evening class at either Piazza Bologna or Eur. I pick up a slice of pizza on the way, which the *pizzaiolo* cuts from a large slab of pizza and hands to me half-wrapped in wax paper. Usually, it keeps me going until classes finish later.

My Italian is improving slowly, although I'll never be a linguist. It's still difficult to engage in a conversation with someone Italian, because as soon as they know I'm an English teacher, they all want to speak English with me. Such is their urgency to learn English.

I came to Rome at a very opportune moment, when English teachers and especially British ones are in demand. I have more work than I can handle and reluctantly have to turn down more teaching work at the school. My private students are the most lucrative. I now have three jobs, teaching at school in the evenings, private lessons in the afternoons and babysitting in the mornings.

How easy it is to be a millionaire in Italy!

Innamorata

Alessandro is never far from my thoughts. We've become very friendly over the last few months.

I often go to Piazza Navona, and invariably he asks one of his fellow artists to look after his stand while he takes me for a glass of wine. If he's busy, he asks me to wait until he finishes later and we have a drink together at the little bar nearby, while the tables and chairs are being stacked up noisily around us.

His English has improved quite considerably, and I like to think that I had a hand in that progress. In fact, his English is now better than my Italian, so we speak mainly in English, with the occasional few words in Italian. I love the way he says my name, *Mar-ga-ret*, with the stress equally on the three syllables, as all my Italian friends do.

I want him to kiss me. I mean REALLY kiss me. Mouth open, probing tongue, and all that, but he is the perfect gentleman and I begin to wonder whether he fancies me or not. Surely a hot-blooded Italian Stallion would have lured me to his bed by now? I become more and more certain that he must be married or in a relationship with someone.

Every time I look at him my heart does a double somersault. I feel like a lovesick teenager.

One evening I pluck up the courage to ask him if he's married.

'*Tu sei sposato?*'

'*Non, cara,*' he replies, looking sad.

Surely he's not gay? I didn't think so, but I ask him anyway.

He laughs. 'No!' and pulls me towards him to plant a kiss firmly on my mouth. Bingo!

He then tells me that he's divorced, with a son, but doesn't have a relationship with the boy's mother any more. He seldom sees his son because he lives with his mother in Sweden. The last time he saw them was when the boy and his mother visited Rome last November.

So, that's who I saw with him. Mystery solved!

I'm relieved, but still haven't got to the bottom of why our relationship has not progressed. Maybe it's because I'm older than him. No problem in my book! Nobody thinks I look my age, and I certainly don't feel it.

'Does it bother you that I'm older than you?' I venture.

'Are you?' is all he says with a twinkle in his eye.

I feel he's playing cat and mouse.

'You have a boyfriend, no?'

I look at him puzzled.

'A boyfriend? No, I don't. What makes you think that?'

'But I see you often, walking with a man in the piazza late at night.'

The penny drops. How could I have been so naïve? He is referring to Frankie. It had not occurred to me that Alessandro might take us for lovers, although our body language might have suggested otherwise. I know Frankie is gay and just assume that everyone else knows too. Really, that was very short-sighted of me, because what I love about Frankie is that he doesn't come across as gay.

I look into Alessandro's dark brown eyes. 'No Alessandro, he's just a friend.'

He grins, kisses me again, and feeling light-headed I wish him '*Buona Notte*' and head home.

In bed I toss and turn. Sleep eludes me. In my head I'm going over the conversation I'd had earlier with Alessandro.

He'd asked me to meet him again tomorrow night for dinner. I couldn't wait.

After school the following night, full of eager anticipation, I take the bus to Piazza Navona.

A light rain has started to fall and the cobblestones glisten in the lamplight. I enter the piazza at the south end, as usual, so it gives me time to take stock before approaching the north end where Alessandro works.

A few artists are still there, packing up their paintings. The object of my desire has spotted me and is striding towards me across the piazza. My heart skips a beat. He's already packed up his stuff and is waiting for me. We embrace and kiss alternate cheeks. I breathe in his scent.

'*Ciao,*' he murmurs softly in my ear. '*Ciao bella.*'

The rain has dampened his hair and it's a mass of curls. A little damp spiral of hair falls down over his forehead. I resist the urge to brush it off his face. What a beautiful man.

We walk out of the piazza, Alessandro pushing a large trolley with all his paintings and equipment on it, towards some large steel containers along the side of the road. They are lock-ups where most of the artists leave their stuff overnight. I'd often wondered about the purpose of these containers.

Alessandro struggles to get all his stuff inside one of them. He has to re-arrange everything several times before he can shut the door. He's being painfully slow, and I'm getting impatient. Eventually, he puts his shoulder against the door and locks it.

A line of motorbikes are parked nearby and Alessandro walks over to one of the more powerful ones.

I hesitate. It's a long time since I've been on a motorbike. Marco and Florence fleetingly pop into my head.

'Don't I need a helmet?' I ask him, stalling for time. Crash helmets are now mandatory in Italy, although lots of youngsters still flaunt the law.

Next minute he reaches into one of his panniers and produces a spare helmet. Obviously, I thought, he's prepared for all eventualities. He helps me to put it on.

'*Carina,*' he grins, his dark eyes twinkling as he fastens the strap under my chin.

'Yes, I'm sure,' I retort sarcastically, being conscious that the helmet is too big for me and I must look like a 'cute' dalek. So much for my hairdo, I think. Throwing caution to the wind, I climb onto the back of the bike.

Off we go. I hold on tightly, with my arms around his waist. I get as close as I can to him and feel the warmth of his hard body against mine.

He turns his head around slightly. He's shouting something to me but the wind blows away his words.

'*Che*?' I yell.

'Why not sit on your own seat?' he yells back.

I hadn't realised that I wasn't sitting on my own pillion seat. In my haste to get as close to him as possible, I'm actually sharing his seat! So I move back. Now there is a big space between our bodies and the chill night air whips around me. I much preferred the other way!

We zoom to the Ponte e Parione, a small, typical Roman *trattoria,* and sit outside under a covered pergola, near a heater that throws out a warm, incandescent glow. Alessandro orders a bottle of red wine and a pasta dish—*Bucatini all' Amatriciana*—his favourite. I love it too. I curl the long pasta around my fork with expertise, and hope that he's suitably impressed!

When we've finished the pasta dish, he asks me if I would like anything else. I am just thinking about *tiramisu*, my favourite dessert, when he suggests *saltimbocca*. I don't know this dessert but it sounds interesting, so I agree and suggest we share one, as I'm quite full from the pasta.

Some minutes later the waitress appears with a plate of pale looking meat and some little roast potatoes. She puts it into the middle of the table. I stare at it. It's not what I was expecting, but I don't say anything. Now I realise that the pasta dish we ate was a *primo piatto*, first course, and this is the *secondo*, or main course. The meat is veal, topped with prosciutto and sage. Alessandro cuts off a piece of meat for me to taste. It's absolutely delicious and just melts in my mouth. Ecstasy!

Alessandro cannot translate *saltimbocca* for me, so I pull out the small pocket dictionary that I always carry with me. The word is derived from the verb *saltare,* to jump and *bocca,* mouth, so it literally means 'jump in the mouth', referring to the delicious explosion of flavour in the mouth.

The rain increases in intensity. We huddle together under

the canopy as it batters onto the canvas. A rose seller is moving around the tables and, as he approaches us, Alessandro pulls some change out of his pocket and buys a crimson rose for me. He orders another bottle of wine.

Maybe it's the wine that does it, but gradually he opens up to me about his personal life. *In vino veritas!*

He tells me that he has a sister with special needs. He gave up his own apartment to live with his mother, so that they could both care for his sister. She needs round the clock care, and requires two carers in order to avoid having to put her into a special home. Now his mother is terminally ill and he is unable to take on the responsibility of both his sister and mother alone. He never mentions his father. His older brother lives in Milan. He's faced with the difficult decision of having to institutionalise his sister.

Alessandro has obviously made many sacrifices, giving up his own apartment and his social life, in order to nurse his sister and, more recently, his mother. Now I understand why it's so difficult for him to have a relationship. The more I know this man, the more I like and respect him. Some people seem to have more than their cross to bear.

Eventually, when the rain eases off, we make a dash for the motorbike and drive off through the cobbled streets. We head around the Piazza Venezia and past the Colosseum in the direction of San Giovanni, to my apartment.

He waits until I get inside the main door and, with a wave, he speeds off into the night.

I'm in love!

BUCATINI ALL'AMATRICIANA
(Alessandro's favourite)

Ingredients:

400 grams bucatini pasta
100 grams lean bacon or pancetta, finely diced
1 onion, finely chopped
2 tablespoons of olive oil
200 grams fresh ripe tomatoes
1 red chilli
70 grams *pecorino* cheese, grated
Salt

Preparation:

Sauté the onion in the oil until it is soft. Add chilli and pancetta and sauté until onion is golden and the pancetta nice and crisp (about 8–10 minutes).

Add tomatoes and cook over a medium heat, stirring occasionally.

Add salt to taste. Remove the chilli.

Cook the pasta *al dente*, drain, and pour into a warm serving bowl or directly into the pan with the sauce.

Mix well, add grated cheese and serve.

Buon Appetito!

Soul Mates

Frankie and I see each other most evenings after school. He knows how I feel about Alessandro. Every time I decide to go to the Piazza to see Alessandro, Frankie acts like he's jealous.

'Forget about him Margarita,' he says. 'Let's go and have some fun.'

Invariably I give in to him, and we just saunter around the centre, maybe cross the bridge into Trastevere, stop and buy a slice of pizza, and watch the boys go by.

Strangely enough we both like the same type. It's as if we're two girlfriends out together. I know he won't pick up anyone while I'm with him. He respects me too much. That's one of the things I like about him.

We spend many weekends together and sometimes I stay over at his place in Piramide, a working class neighbourhood in Testaccio, known for its authentic Roman cuisine. He has a small, but comfortable, one-bedroom apartment. He gives up his bed for me and sleeps on the floor.

Often I tell him he can sleep with me, but I always get the same response, an emphatic NO! I kid myself that maybe he's not really gay and that he'll suddenly pounce on me. I know I'm banging my head against a brick wall, but I live in hope! I'm sure that if Frankie had been heterosexual we would be much more than friends. We are soul mates. We have become almost inseparable and, I would imagine, appear to be a loving couple to most people.

Frankie is very tactile. We hug and kiss, and link arms as we walk along the streets together. Sometimes I feel like I'm looking at a mirror image of myself. Kindred spirits. Heather says we are 'one soul'.

When Frankie gets some acting work, I help him to rehearse his lines. We have great fun. He loves to cook, and we spend a lot of time together in his kitchen, making his favourite *Penne all' Arrabbiata*.

Sometimes, other friends come over and join us for dinner, and we all sit around talking into the early hours. If we feel like an ice cream at midnight, we all troop across the road to the *gelateria* and hang around in the warm summer air, until the road cleaners come by.

If I stay over with Chris Frankie gets his knickers in a twist and wants to know what I see in him.

'Well Frankie,' I say, looking directly at him, 'until I get a better offer…'

He huffs and puffs. Of course, he knows what I'm getting at!

'*Madonna*, Margarita, how many more times, don't drive me crazy!'

He doesn't realise how crazy he's making me feel. I have to tread on eggshells when dealing with him. He has such a short fuse.

Whenever I try to converse with Frankie in Italian for some practice, he gets very impatient with me and we usually end up having an argument. I'm not going to learn any Italian from him.

He's a bit of an eccentric. We fight a lot. There's always some drama production!

One night we're having drinks at Shelter, a drinking club that we often go to, and after another of his outbursts he flounces out of the bar. I've really had enough of him acting like a prima donna, so later that night at home I compose a letter to him. I don't know whether I will actually send it to him or not, but it makes me feel better just writing my thoughts and feelings down. In it, I blame him for my emotional confusion, that he is giving me mixed messages with regard to his feelings towards me. I finish the letter by saying that perhaps we shouldn't see each other for a while. Then I put it in my bag, deciding that I will read it again tomorrow, before making up my mind whether or not to send it to him.

The following morning I'm in the Villa Borghese near cats' corner, when I see Frankie enter the gates of the park. He strides over to me, and without saying a word, hands me an envelope.

'What's this?' I ask him.

'It's a letter. I want you to read it after I've left and you can tell me what you think tonight after school,' he responds. He looks very serious.

I hesitate, wondering if I should give him the letter that's in my bag, but I want a chance to read his letter first, then I'll decide whether to give it to him or not.

'Well, it so happens I've got a letter for you too,' I hesitate, 'but I've left it at home. I was going to hand it to you tonight at school,' I lie.

'Okay, then bring it tonight, and don't change anything,' he warns me, as if he knows what I'm up to. Then he leaves. I am dying to open the letter, but want to wait until I'm alone. So I put it in my pocket to read later.

After I leave Susanna's house I can't wait any longer. I have an hour before my private lesson with Marra, so I walk up to Aphrodite, the little bar on the corner of the piazza, and order a *cappuccino* (even though it is after 11 a.m. and no Italian would drink cappuccino after that time). Frankie has suggested that in order to get a hot coffee, I should ask for *acqua bollente,* boiling water. Although the *barista* gives me a strange look and repeats '*Acqua bollente per la signora!*' for the whole bar to hear, it does arrive hot!

I open the letter.

> *Cara M*
> *I can't explain my feelings towards you as I've never felt love for a woman before. I enjoy being with you and when I don't see you I miss you very much.*
>
> *I'm sorry for my outburst the other night, but sometimes you stifle me Margaret. We're going round in circles. I know you want something from me that I can't give.*

So perhaps we should cool it a bit and not see each other for a while. I need to sort out my feelings.
I love you.
F

Ditto!

He had written an almost identical letter to mine!

I read it over again twice, trying to read between the lines, trying to make something out of nothing. It's true, I do want something from him that I know he can't give, but I just won't accept it.

Maybe it's time to face up to the fact that we'll never be more than friends. No matter how much time and attention he gives me he's not going to fall in love with me.

I decide not to give him my letter.

That evening when I see him at school in EUR he asks me for the letter.

'I've ripped it up,' I lie. 'Anyway, it said more or less the same as yours, and I agree, we do need a break.'

Over the next few days Frankie avoids me like the plague, but eventually we gravitate back to each other and to our usual routine. Because we're soul mates!

Frankie is a very private person but gradually he confides in me about his life. He was born in Naples. His mother and father were not married. When his father chose not to recognise Frankie as his legitimate son, his mother placed Frankie in an orphanage that was run by priests. He was sexually abused. Several times he ran away.

I am outraged.

'Didn't you tell anyone?'

'No,' he answers.

'What about your mother, didn't you tell her?' I'm incredulous.

'Yes, I tried but she accused me of lying, beat me and sent me back to the orphanage. The priest was the only person who showed me any kindness and I didn't know any different.'

I feel tears prickle my eyes.

He continues to tell me his story. When he was sixteen, he left the institution and headed for the port, where he found work on a ship that was bound for Bermuda. He settled on the island for a number of years, obtaining work in restaurants. It was in Bermuda that he met Eugene and they became good friends.

Wanting to trace his roots and hoping to eventually find his father, Frankie decided to return to Italy and travelled to Naples to locate his mother. She was no longer at the address he remembered. After several days of making enquiries from neighbours, he had eventually managed to locate her. They were like complete strangers to each other, but she was able to give him some information as to the possible whereabouts of his father who, she believed, was still alive and living just outside Naples. So far, he had done nothing with the information.

'I want to visit him now,' he says to me.

I have misgivings about him just turning up unannounced, but I volunteer to go with him for moral support.

'Thanks, but it's something I need to do on my own,' he replies.

'Well, alright, but be prepared that you may be disappointed,' I warn him.

The next day he leaves for Naples.

Several days later I receive a telephone call from him. He's just arrived back in Rome, so we arrange to meet at Pizzeria Forum. I have a shock when I see him.

'What happened?' I'm concerned about how tired and drawn he looks.

Between gulps of red wine he tells me that when he arrived at the address he'd been given, which was an isolated farmhouse in the countryside, he had come face to face with a man holding a shotgun!

When Frankie tried to explain who he was, the man ordered him off his land calling him 'the son of the devil.'

The man holding the shotgun was his mother's brother, Frankie's uncle.

His uncle's wife saw what was happening, intervened and invited Frankie into the house for something to eat. Frankie's father was not living with them but she was able to give Frankie his father's telephone number.

It took Frankie a couple of days to pluck up the courage to telephone his father who, according to Frankie was polite but cool. He would not agree to meet up with Frankie, although they spoke for some time on the phone.

It was a very painful experience for Frankie, but it closed a chapter in his life.

Another birthday!

I'm teaching at EUR this evening. Luana comes to class bearing gifts and invites me for lunch at the weekend.

After we've finished teaching, Frankie and I meet for dinner at the restaurant in the park. Handing me a parcel, he kisses me lightly on the lips, and wishes me *'Buon compleanno.'* His gift is a statue of an angel that changes colour according to the weather, pink for fine and blue for rain. It's rather pretty.

Arriving back at the apartment, the telephone is ringing as I open the door. It's Chris. He wants to take me to Umbria at the weekend for my birthday. I agree to go. I telephone Luana to give her my apologies about lunch and promise to drop by when I return.

On Saturday, Chris picks me up from my apartment in his convertible. He has the roof down, and music blasts from the tape player. Although the weather is a little nippy, we're nice and cosy in the car.

We head north on the autostrada out of Rome towards Umbria, passing many picturesque hilltop towns along the way. I promise myself that one day I will explore some of them.

We make a photo stop in the small commune of San Gemini, a picturesque medieval town, well known for its mineral water springs. We walk around the tangled maze of alleyways and find a small 'hole in the wall' *trattoria* within the city walls. An ornate clock graces the faded and peeling rose-coloured exterior of the building. A small bell tower sits on the roof. Inside, the dining area is very small with only a few tables. There are no menus. The owner, who is also the chef, appears at our table and proceeds to tell us what we will be eating! It's a mouth-watering Umbrian delicacy, pasta with truffles.

Back on the road after a very satisfying lunch, we head for Todi, another well preserved hilltop town, where we collect a dozen bottles of local wine from the Cantina Sociale Tudernum. The winery lies amidst the vineyards on the sloping hills of Todi, and customers fill their empty bottles from large vats that look like petrol pumps. The clock on the wine pump registers the amount of wine and the cost. We have a choice of *Vino Rosato, Vino Rosso, Vino Bianco and Vino Grechetto*, all for less than 2000 lire a litre!

Well stocked with Vini Tudernum, we continue our journey listening to Laura Pausini, a popular Italian singer. We're heading for Stefano's sprawling farmhouse in the countryside, near Todi.

Stefano and his wife Ella, make us very welcome. They both speak excellent English. Stefano is an artist and sculptor. I find him a very attractive and interesting man, and although his artwork isn't my cup of tea, he is extremely talented.

We spend a very enjoyable evening talking well into the wee small hours, before we all retire. Even though there are four bedrooms, Ella has no compunction about offering Chris and I a double room.

However, we've had so much to drink, that we just cuddle together, which is really rather nice!

The next day, after a flying visit to Perugia, the university town where the streets are full of young people, we head back to Rome. Chris drops me off at Luana's house, where I spend a couple of hours with her and her husband Gianni, and then I leave, heading back to the centre.

Franca is throwing a small party in my honour at her apartment. Chris comes along to give me some moral support, as I feel very intimidated by Franca's erudite friends. Although my Italian has improved tremendously, I still find it difficult to enter into a debate and express an opinion in Italian. It takes me too long to think of the right words and, by the time I have, the conversation has moved on!

The party breaks up just after midnight and Chris drops me back home.

A New Apartment

Eugene is finding it difficult to get work. He does not have a *Permesso di Soggiorno*, and his visa has run out.

'Margarita,' he says to me one evening, 'I'm going home daahling. It's so bloody difficult to get work here.'

I'm devastated. First Gayle and now Eugene. I try to talk him out of it, but he's adamant. Personally, I don't think Eugene is cut out for teaching. He is more suited to the fashion industry, or hospitality.

It also means that I now have to find another flat-mate.

I'm already getting a little tired of the apartment. It has its advantages, such as the private bathroom and the courtyard, but it also has its disadvantages.

Situated on the ground floor of a high apartment block, my room doesn't get much sunlight, and can be quite dark in the winter months. Also, the building is nine-storeys high, so there are eight flats directly above ours. Two of these apartments in particular have no compunction about throwing all sorts of debris out of their windows, which lands in our courtyard. The worst problem is cigarette butts. Lots of people still smoke in Italy, and sometimes while sitting in our garden a cigarette butt comes sailing down from above, narrowly missing our drinks or food if we are eating outside.

Gabriella knew who was responsible, and once became so incensed with all the dog-ends landing in our garden, that she gathered them up and left them on the culprit's doorstep! The problem ceased, but for only a short time.

We also have various items of laundry floating down from above, as residents tend to hang their washing from lines on the outside of their balconies. Some of the lines are on pulleys, fixed from one balcony to another.

Occasionally, we find a pair of panties or other item of clothing caught up in our lemon tree.

So now that Eugene is leaving, maybe it's time for me to change apartments again. This time I'm determined to find a big apartment for myself and rent out one or two rooms.

Once again I turn to *Wanted in Rome*, a good investment for 1,000 lire. Where would all the expats be without it? This time I find an advertisement for a large, three-bedroom apartment in Via F. Gregorovius, a residential area, not far from where I am currently living. Ideal.

> Macedonia—Fully furnished apt. 4th floor, Lift. 150 sq. mtrs. 3 bedrooms, 2 bathrooms. Large living room. Kitchen. 2 balconies. Telephone. L2,000,000 monthly Tel: 7886557.

I call the number and speak to the advertiser, a lady, who speaks perfect English with an accent that is definitely not Italian. We arrange a mutually convenient time for me to view the apartment later that afternoon.

I ask Frankie and Eugene to come with me to look at it. It would be fantastic if we could all move in together. We walk from Via Caulonia, across the railway bridge, and down Via Macedonia until we reach an apartment block surrounded by a high, stone wall with wrought-iron entrance gates. The building is four-storeys high and the top apartment has a roof garden. The walls are ochre-washed, with green roller shutters at the windows and a balcony that runs the whole length of the building.

We walk through a garden stocked with exotic plants and shrubs to the front entrance where the owner, who turns out to be German, is waiting to show us around.

It's such a beautiful apartment. As soon as I enter the spacious hallway, I know I've found what I want. A vase of freshly-cut flowers stands on an antique wooden chest that sits against one wall. Shiny black Italian marble tiles cover the floors and there is a pleasant aroma of polish. The rooms are large and airy and full of antique furniture. A grand old oak table in the dining area would easily seat fourteen people. In the lounge area the leather sofas are old, but squashy and comfortable, and the floor in here is also tiled. A terrace runs the whole length of the apartment on both sides. The French windows of the lounge, dining room and two bedrooms open onto the front terrace, which although too narrow for a table and chairs, is lined with terracotta pots filled with colourful plants and shrubs. The kitchen opens out onto the rear terrace.

There are three bedrooms and two bathrooms. The two main bedrooms are well decorated and furnished with double beds, but the slightly smaller bedroom is dominated by a huge carved antique chest, so will only take a single bed. There are built-in bookcases on two walls, which are completely full of large volume books. I guess this was used originally as the study. French windows lead out onto the balcony.

I absolutely fall in love with the apartment, and although the rent is high, I know that if I lease out two bedrooms I can just about afford it.

Next to the apartment building there is a small market with a few stalls selling fresh produce and, of course, the mandatory flower-stall.

On Via Macedonia there is a *macelleria* selling *carne fresche*, a butcher selling fresh meat. *Carne* is not to be confused with *cane* which means dog! The pronunciation is very similar. There's also a bar, a *tabbachaio*, and a *gelateria*. Everything I need!

After some negotiations with the landlady, who turns out to be a real gem, I manage to secure a slightly reduced rent of 1,700,000 per month. It's the done thing to barter. She invites me to her apartment in San Giovanni later that evening to sign the *Contratto di Locazione*.

Now it is my turn to advertise in *Wanted in Rome*.

> Wanted—2 people m/f to share luxury fully furnished apartment with one professional lady.

3 bedrooms, 2 bathrooms, large living room, 2 balconies, eat-in kitchen, Call Margaret on 7005968.

I have a dozen replies and narrow it down to five applicants.

Allison is a student from America. She's been in Rome for a year and will be studying here for another year. Her Sicilian boyfriend is in the *Carabinieri*, the Italian Military police force. A long-legged blonde, she has a lovely personality and speaks fluent Italian.

Eileen is an Irish girl working at La FAO, the same organisation that Dawn works for. Eileen has recently returned from Rwanda. Because of all the atrocities she had witnessed while working there, she now has a desk job for two years and is undergoing therapy. This, apparently, is normal procedure. She tells me that between April and June this year an estimated 800,000 people were massacred in the Rwandan genocide. Eileen has seen horrors that will never be erased from her memory.

Marie is from England and works in a bar. She's a pleasant girl, but younger than I would like as a flatmate.

Camilla is also from England and teaches English at The British Council. She looks down her nose when I tell her that I teach at a private school.

Antoinetta is from the north of Italy and currently studying to become a doctor. She speaks very little English.

It's a difficult decision to make as I feel comfortable with all of them, with the possible exception of Camilla. I feel that Marie is too immature, and as I really need to brush up on my Italian, I should probably choose Antoinetta.

In the end I go with my gut instincts.

I decide on Eileen and Allison, and arrange to meet them with Signora De Luca at the apartment one evening to show them around.

Over the next few days it's 'all hands on deck' as Luana, Frankie and Chris, all help me to move my stuff from Via Caulonia. At the end of November, Eileen and Allison move in with me.

It was to prove an excellent arrangement.

I've come to the conclusion that the drivers in Rome are some of the best in the world. How many drivers can park in the tight spaces that Romans can? How do they manage to manoeuvre their cars along the narrow *vicolos*, or around the Piazza Venezia without incident? Six roads converge into this piazza and there are no traffic lights. At rush hour, *ora di punta*, a white-gloved traffic policeman, *vigile,* stands on a little round podium situated in the middle of the piazza directing the traffic like a conductor directing a symphony. It's such a spectacle that tourists sit at the pavement cafes around the piazza watching the show!

As far as Romans are concerned the pavement is to park on. It's almost impossible to walk along without having to step into the road to circumnavigate the parked vehicles.

Crossing a road with pedestrian lights, the pedestrian has right of way when the green sign lights up with *avanti*. If, however, you need to cross the road at a crossing without pedestrian lights, and there are many of them, you wait forever, as no driver stops for a pedestrian. Here the driver has right of way. Just step out into the road and you may think you are risking life and limb, but lo and behold, you reach the other side without mishap, as the cars just go around you.

Gayle and I used to joke about waiting for a nun or a woman with a child so that we could cross the road safely with them. After a while I found that the trick is to look confident, stride out quickly, don't dither and the drivers will manoeuvre around you rather than hit you! He who hesitates is lost. Having said that, however, on average seven pedestrians are involved in accidents with scooters or cars every day in Rome.

One evening, Franca invites me to a concert given by the Accademia di Santa Cecilia symphony orchestra, with Daniele Gatti conducting. It's an excellent performance and after a quick nightcap at Bramptons, Franca insists on taking me home.

We are driving around Piazza Venezia when a bus cuts in front of us and hits the car. Franca stays in her car and the bus driver, looking absolutely furious, approaches us. There follows a tirade of arguing, of which I understand very little. Franca explains that they have to wait for the police. Her car is still driveable, but neither of the vehicles can move until the police arrive.

We sit for a while and nothing happens. The driver of the bus is sitting at his wheel, occasionally gesticulating at other irate drivers who need to get around us, since we are on a corner.

Finally, Franca suggests that I take a taxi home before it gets too late. I feel reluctant to leave her by herself, but it seems the sensible thing to do, so I walk around the corner to the taxi rank to find a cab. Taxi cabs are not hailed on the street here as they can be in London. I climb into the only cab on the rank and as it turns the corner of the piazza, I catch a glimpse of Franca sitting in her car, still waiting for the police.

Pollution in Rome is high. This is in part because it lies in a valley between the seven hills, Capitoline, Palatine, Aventine, Caelian, Esquiline, Quirinal and Viminal. The pollution hangs over the valley until the *tramontana*—literally translated to 'between the mountains'—the brisk wind from the north which frequents the city in winter, disperses it.

There is a high incidence of respiratory infections, including pneumonia from high levels of pollution, mostly from motor traffic.

The city has a particularly clever law. Cars are allowed into the centre of the city on alternate days, depending on the registration plate. For instance, all cars with odd numbered registrations are allowed into the centre on one day, and cars with even numbered registrations the following day, and so on. This has helped to cut pollution. Heavy fines are imposed if you take your car into the centre on the wrong day.

Unfortunately, the public transport system is inadequate to transport the extra people on the days when they cannot drive in.

Chaos reigns supreme!

Most cities in Italy have the first two letters of the city on the car registration plate, Fi is *Firenze*, Mi is *Milano* etc. In Rome, the registration plate has the complete name, *Roma*.

S.P.Q.R.!

On my many walks around Rome I often come across the letters S.P.Q.R.

When I ask Frankie what it stands for, he grins and says, *Sono Pazzi Questi Romani*, They are Crazy these Romans. In truth, it stands for *Senatus Populus Que Romanus,* which is Latin for The Senate and People of Rome.

The slang translation is not meant to be derogatory to the Romans, but is yet another dig at their superiority complex!

This year I've decided to spend Christmas and New Year in Rome. Frankie will be going to his adopted family in Castel Gandolfo for a few days, as usual.

In Piazza Navona, the annual Christmas market with stalls selling Christmas goodies, fairy lights, sweets, *biscotti, torrone* (nougat with almonds and honey) and toys for children will be open until the sixth of January. Alessandro will be working in Piazza Navona on the Christmas stalls.

Chris will be singing in the choir at midnight mass in St Peter's this year.

Franca has invited me to stay with her over Christmas, so after dinner at her place on Christmas Eve we'll go to mass together. I arrive at her apartment that afternoon, bearing flowers, chocolates and wine.

The traditional Christmas Eve dinner is fish. Franca makes *capitone,* roasted eel. Once I get over what it is, I find it rather tasty.

Around ten o'clock we leave for the Pantheon, a historic temple in Piazza della Rotonda and an enormous reminder of the ancient splendour of Rome. Franca tells me that when it rains you can watch the raindrops floating down through the gaping oculus in the dome, splattering onto the worn marble flooring and flowing away through the drain on the floor. Tonight it doesn't rain, but it's a magical night.

After the midnight mass, Franca and I walk back to her apartment. A mist has risen from the river and permeates through the streets, swirling eerily around us like wisps of smoke.

We link arms and hurry home, our high heels beat out a

staccato rhythm on the cobblestones, echoing through the damp, deserted streets.

At noon on Christmas Day, the Pope gives his traditional blessing and Christmas message from the steps of St Peter's. Cries of '*Viva il Papa*' ring out. Franca and I watch the event on the television and spend the rest of the day relaxing together.

Frascati is a wine region thirty-four kilometres east of Rome. It's the most beautiful town of the Castelli Romani. The hillside is covered with magnificent villas, where many of the rich and famous used to live.

Franca has been invited to a dinner party for New Year's Eve, *La Notte di San Silvestro* or *Capodanno*, and she can take a friend. She asks me if I'd like to go with her.

'Wouldn't you rather take a man,' I tease her.

Franca and I share similar opinions of men. Although we both enjoy the company of men, we are just as happy and comfortable in the company of women.

I feel a little trepidation, as I know I will be completely out of my depth with her friends. Apart from the fact that they are all academics, the main topics of discussion will be Italian politics, literature and football. However, if I am to improve my Italian, I must mix with the locals, so I accept her invitation.

We take the Via Tuscolana to Frascati. Her friends live in one of the beautiful villas on the hillside. Margut is Polish. She is a very striking-looking woman of about fifty, with great bone structure and, like Franca, a psychologist. Her Italian husband Giorgio is a plastic surgeon, dealing mainly with criminal injuries. I can't help wondering if her fantastic cheekbones are down to him.

They speak a little English and do so for my benefit for a while, but soon lapse into Italian. I cannot understand the finer points, although I get the gist of what they are saying.

Another guest arrives. Franca knows Mauritzio, and I get the impression that her friends are match making!

With elections looming on the horizon, the conversation quickly turns to politics.

Silvio Berlusconi formed *Forza Italia*, a centre-right party in 1993, and looks set to win the elections. He is a self-made man, one of Italy's richest, and owns TV networks and the AC Milan football team.

In Italy people discuss and take sides publicly on their political views. Lively discussions take place and I feel very inadequate that I cannot voice an opinion in Italian. It's all very frustrating, but makes me all the more determined to learn this romantic language.

We celebrate the New Year with a traditional dinner of lentils, symbolic of money and good fortune, followed by *zampone*, which are stuffed pigs' trotters, and drink in the New Year with *prosecco*, sparkling white wine.

Franca and I are invited to stay overnight and considering the amount of wine we've consumed, we gratefully accept.

We make an early start back to Rome the following morning, stopping in the small town of Ariccia, famous for its *porchetta*, roast pig stuffed with herbs. We cannot resist the succulent aroma that wafts over to us, so we buy a sandwich from one of the roadside stalls.

Handing us our hot *panini*, the vendor wishes us *Felice Anno Nuovo*, Happy New Year. It's 1995.

Latin Lover

I love Piazza Navona all year round, but one of my favourite times is in the winter when the air is cold and crisp, when all the tourists have gone home, and only a handful of artists are there. It is on such a winter's night that I meet up with Alessandro.

It's late and the piazza is almost deserted, the bars and restaurants are all closed, and the tables and chairs are stacked. Most of the artists have already left.

There is a solitary figure walking towards me across the piazza. It's Alessandro. I feel my legs turning to jelly. He's so drop-dead gorgeous.

'*Ciao,*' he greets me, with his crooked smile.

My heart skips a beat.

'*Ciao Alessandro.*'

We stand looking at each other for what seems like an eternity.

'*Andiamo,* let's go for a drink.'

He takes my hand and we walk out of the piazza, through the narrow cobbled streets, until we arrive at a small bar. He is greeted by several of the customers. I feel flattered that he is comfortable enough with me to bring me into his local. He orders a bottle of red wine. I enjoy a glass or two, but after the third glass, I feel quite tipsy. A warm glow spreads through my body. At that moment Alessandro suddenly grabs my hand and pulls me towards him. His lips are warm and soft on mine. I feel dizzy. I close my eyes.

The next moment we're on our feet and out of the bar. He stops further down the street in front of a large wooden door, opens it and we step inside.

> *We don't say a word as we tear each other's clothes off. We fall upon the bed. His breath is hot on my face. We kiss and caress each other slowly. He kisses my eyes, my lips, gently at first then fiercely, his touch sending shivers through my whole body. I let out a moan as he traces his tongue gently down my body. He enters me swiftly, our bodies moving together in perfect unison in an ever increasing crescendo. I had waited for this moment for ever.*
>
> *'Tu sei bella,' he murmurs into my hair. 'Ti amo.'*

'HELLO!'

I am back in the bar. Alessandro is looking at me expectantly.

'*Mi dispiace.*' I stammer. '*Che hai detto?*' I ask him what he'd said, while I was in cloud cuckoo land.

'Shall we go?' he repeats.

That's a bit ambiguous I think to myself, go where?

'OK,' I reply.

Leaving the bar we walk hand in hand to his motorbike. We head along the Fiori Imperiale, past the Colosseum in the direction of San Giovanni to my apartment.

I wonder whether to invite him inside. When I interviewed the girls to share my apartment, I made a rule that no men could stay overnight. I certainly didn't want to bump into a strange man in my apartment early in the morning. Allison sometimes stayed over with her boyfriend, Andrea, at his place. Eileen didn't have a boyfriend and didn't seem interested anyway, and I thought that if I met someone he would have his own apartment.

But in Italy rules are made to be broken, so I invite Alessandro in for a drink anyway. He hesitates, says it's too late and maybe some other time.

Waiting until I get inside the building, he blows me kiss as he drives off.

Is he *never* going to be my Latin Lover?

Death's Door

In winter, the temperature in Rome can sometimes be colder than the temperature in London.

My classes often finish late in the evenings, and by the time I arrive at Piazza Venezia to wait for a connecting bus to my apartment, the cold and dampness is seeping into the ancient stones of the city, and into my bones.

If I stand with my back to the Museum wall, I can feel a little warm air emanating from a grill set down low in the wall. I always make a bee-line for this particular spot, but usually someone has beaten me to it.

Arriving at Piazza Venezia one Monday night from the school in Piazza Bologna, the wind is particularly cold. The minutes tick by and no bus is materialising. I've bagged the grill, but it only warms the back of my legs and I can't stop shivering. Eventually, after about twenty minutes the bus arrives, and thankfully I climb on.

After several of these extremely cold and damp February nights, I go down with what I think is 'flu. I stay in bed for the whole weekend, feeling sorry for myself and dosing myself with a variety of 'flu remedies, hoping to nip it in the bud.

On Monday morning I drag myself out of bed to go to Susanna's. I bump into Eileen in the kitchen.

'Oh, my God!' she exclaims when she sees me. 'You look awful. Have you seen yourself?'

I look in the mirror and get a shock. I hardly recognise the grey, drawn face staring back at me, through red-rimmed eyes. It's scary! 'You look like death warmed up' my mother would have said.

'Go back to bed,' Eileen orders. 'I'll call Susanna and the school and let them know you won't be in.'

I don't protest too much when she ushers me back into bed. My legs are shaking so much I can hardly stand, and I'm coughing up blood.

Eileen also calls Frankie, who calls round later with medicine. He has some acting work lined up and goes over his script, while keeping me company for the evening.

Two days later and I'm still no better. I have a temperature. There's no way I can get to a doctor's surgery. I'm as weak as a kitten. Eileen calls in her doctor from La FAO. After a thorough examination, he advises me to have a chest X-ray at the hospital, as soon as possible. He prescribes a course of antibiotics for three days. Meanwhile, I must stay in bed, and going to work is out of the question.

'Is there anyone who can look after you?' he enquires. 'Otherwise I can arrange for you to be admitted into hospital.'

That was the last resort in my opinion.

Eileen and Allison would be around, but I didn't want to have to rely on them. Franca was away on business in the north of Italy, and Frankie was now busy in rehearsals. I could only think of one person who would have the time and the inclination to do it. Luana. I ask Eileen to call Luana who immediately promises to come over the next day.

True to her word, she arrives the following morning with homemade soup, and fusses around me like a mother hen.

'I'll come tomorrow and take you to the hospital for your X-rays,' she says. I am too weak to argue and just thankful that she's around.

The following morning she comes around eleven o'clock. I still feel weak but I have stopped coughing up blood. My chest is very painful. We drive to San Giovanni Hospital. After a long wait I am called in to see a doctor. They will only take X-rays if I stay in the hospital as a patient. I can think of nothing worse. I refuse, much to Luana's consternation, so she then decides to take me straight to her doctor in EUR, who sends me for X-rays to a radiologist nearby.

After my X-rays, Luana takes me home and tucks me up in bed, promising to return the following day to take me back to the doctor for the results.

I am diagnosed with bronchial pneumonia and given another course of stronger antibiotics, and told to stay in bed.

Luana comes every day for the next two weeks, bringing her tasty homemade soup, which she feeds to me like a baby!

Day by day I slowly improve, thanks to her care, until I'm strong enough to look after myself and eventually return to work.

I will never forget the kindness of Luana, and I truly believe she saved my life.

My bout of pneumonia has set me back a few weeks and I haven't been able to see Alessandro. I've missed him.

When I eventually get to the Piazza, I do my usual detour to suss out the situation before approaching him. He's sitting alone on the stone bench near his stand. Suddenly I feel shy.

He spots me, looks surprised and then his face breaks into a smile. He seems delighted to see me.

'*Dov'e andata?*' He wants to know where I've been.

I try to explain. Whether he fully understands or not, I don't know, but the big bear-like hug he gives me is all the medicine I need!

Alessandro takes my hand, '*mi sei mancata*' which means that he missed me.

'*Anch' io.*' I tell him that I've missed him too. Could we be making progress?

I've decided to conform and buy a mobile telephone, a *telefonino*. I realised when I was ill and unable to get out of bed what a godsend it would have been.

Although Alessandro has a *telefonino* I've never asked him for the number. If I want to see him I just turn up at the piazza. I have no address or contact number for him, so he could just disappear off the face of the earth and I wouldn't know where or how to find him. When I mentioned this to him he replied: 'I am always here *come una lampada*,' like a lamp-post!

Everywhere I go in Rome there is the omnipresent shrill of the *telefonini*, if they are not already clamped to an ear. It is a necessary accessory. Sometimes when I'm on the bus a mobile will ring and, simultaneously, several people reach for their phones. I find it quite amusing.

Now I'll be doing the same!

Luana and I have become firm friends since my pneumonia scare. I'm invited regularly to their house for lunch at weekends. I take the train from Termini to Magliana Station where either Luana or Gianni meet me in their little blue Fiat *Cinquecento* (my favourite Italian word, pronounced 'chinkwachento', and means five-hundred), to drive me to their home for lunch. While I'm waiting, I watch the graffiti-covered trains pass through the station.

Luana and Gianni live in a gated apartment block in Torre di Valle in the south of Rome. Their modern apartment is very spacious, light and airy. Sometimes, weather permitting we eat lunch on their small balcony overlooking the well-kept communal gardens. Luana always serves a delicious meal and makes a fuss of me, as usual.

After lunch, Luana brings out the *limoncello*, the digestive drink, which she makes herself. I accept a small glass of the sweet sticky lemon liqueur, but still cannot find anything pleasant about it.

Luana insists that we all have a *siesta*. Ushering me into her study where there is a single divan, she closes the shutters and curtains so that not a chink of light penetrates into the room, and closes the door.

'*Dormi bene,*' she calls as she leaves the room.

I find it a rather strange thing to do with a visitor, but it's their routine, and in a way I am flattered that they feel comfortable enough to treat me as one of them.

Although I am not particularly tired, I always manage to fall asleep very quickly, probably due to the amount of wine I've consumed over lunch! I awake feeling refreshed and revitalised, unlike when I have an afternoon nap on the sofa at home. Maybe the secret is to have a good lunch with wine first.

Luana is like a colourful butterfly, always immaculately groomed in seasonal colours. I feel quite dull and sombre beside her as I favour more neutral colours.

We're shopping buddies and she knows where all the best bargains are to be found. Little by little her influence rubs off on me, and I become more adventurous with colours.

Gianni also dresses quite flamboyantly and I come to the conclusion that only in Italy could men get away with such bright colours. They wear their clothes with a panache that British men do not have. It's also fashionable for men to carry a *borsellino*, a handbag for men!

Just try asking an Englishman to put on a pale lemon jacket with black shirt and trousers and carry a handbag!

The average Roman woman is extremely well groomed. Appearance is very important. *La Bella Figura* is all about creating a good image. Italians are very conscious of how they dress and present themselves.

Franca never ceases to amaze me. She transforms herself in just a few minutes and looks absolutely stunning, as if she'd spent hours on her appearance. She seems to do it with very little effort. She owns three mink coats and wears them with style. The demise of the fur coat just hasn't happened in Rome!

The women are also regimented and have cut-off dates for seasonal clothes, whatever the temperature.

For example at the end of April, come rain or shine, off come the black stockings and on go the pale fishnet tights. Then at the end of October reverse the procedure! If you don't adhere to this pattern, you are not considered to have *La Bella Figura*.

When I first arrived in Rome, I wore dark tights as the weather in England had turned quite cool. In Rome, however, the weather was still very warm and the Italian girls were still wearing pale tights, as the change-over date had not arrived. I looked quite incongruous. I also wore stiletto heels, picking my way unsteadily over the cobblestones. I very quickly swopped them for a pair of stylish flats. I'm amazed how the Italian girls manage to walk on the cobblestones in their stiletto heels, but they do, and with style.

And there is not a training shoe in sight!

On the Via del Governo Vecchio I discover three *abiti usato*, second-hand or vintage shops. Being a bit of a second-hand Rose, I spend a whole afternoon exploring them. I buy a pair of Levi jeans, which would normally cost 120,000 lire, for 40,000 lire. I feel very pleased with myself.

The longer I stay in Rome the more I try to follow the local fashion. Gianni's mother, Elena, is always commenting on how *elegante* I look. I try to blend in as much as possible, adopting the current fashion trends, colour, and could possibly, at a stretch, pass for an Italian of northern origin, who are much paler skinned and have light eyes.

Walking through Piazza Navona one evening, two young men, *ragazzi*, pass me. We make eye contact and one of them remarks, '*Che begli occhi*', what beautiful eyes. The Italians are fascinated by green eyes.

LUANA'S RECIPE FOR LIMONCELLO

Ingredients:

1 kilogram lemons
1 litre alcohol, 90% proof
1 kilogram sugar
1 litre water

Preparation:

Wash and dry the lemons.

Peel the skin from the lemons, taking care there is no pith. In a large jar add the alcohol and lemon skin. Cover the jar and leave for about ten days, until the liquid becomes yellow.

Put the water and sugar in a saucepan and place over a low heat, stirring until the sugar has dissolved. Allow to cool before adding it to the *limoncello* mixture.

After the rest period, strain the mixture and discard the lemon peel.

Pour into bottles and place in freezer.

Serve in frosted liqueur glasses after lunch or dinner!

Salute!

ZUPPA DI LUANA

Slice some celery, carrots, and onion and slowly bring to boil in a vegetable broth.

Add in some little macaroni pasta.

Add salt and pepper to taste and serve up piping hot to sick friends!

Buon salute!

Guardia Di Finanza

The *Guardia di Finanza,* appear at the school in Re di Roma one Friday evening. Although they have Military status, unlike the *Carabinieri* it is part of the Italian Armed Forces under the authority of the minister of Economy and Finance. Its aim is to prevent, investigate and report fraud, tax evasion and money laundering, illegal immigration and Mafia operations.

It seems they have been alerted by an ex-employee that the school is employing teachers who are working illegally, and paying them 'under the table' to avoid taxes. The ex-employee was fired from the school, so obviously has an axe to grind.

The *Guardia* are questioning Antonella, the receptionist on the front desk. They want to check the company's books.

Antonella tries to explain to them that the director, Signor Ottomanelli, is not available and that only he has access to the books. The *Guardia* will not leave and insist on seeing Ottomanelli, or being put in touch with him.

I am at the school to collect my last two weeks' wages. I feel sorry for the poor girl. She picks up the telephone and dials Ottomanelli's number. There is no reply.

The *Guardia* are quite formidable. Dressed in grey and navy military-style uniform and carrying guns, they are not to be messed with. They want to go into Ottomanelli's office. Antonella reluctantly lets them in

'Stay in there with them,' I hiss, 'and I'll keep trying Nicolas' who, as usual, is *incommunicado.*

The *Guardia* go through everything, and eventually emerge carrying armfuls of files, which they confiscate. A tearful Antonella watches them leave.

'That's me out of a job,' she sobs.

I don't say as much, but I think that's all of us out of a job.

I am right. The following Monday evening when I turn up at the school in Piazza Bologna, the door is locked and there is no-one to be seen. A sign on the door reads: CLOSED UNTIL FURTHER NOTICE. There is no signature.

Is the school in EUR also closed I wonder? I dial their number on my mobile.

I get a recorded message:

'You have reached Studio Cassino. Due to unforseen circumstances we are closed until further notice.'

The line went dead. There was no opportunity to leave a message.

Frankie should be teaching tonight at EUR, so I phone him.

'*Pronto* Margarita.'

'I assume you've been to the school and found them closed?'

'Yes, I don't know what the hell's going on.'

I tell him about the visit from the *Guardia* at Re di Roma last Friday.

'They must have found something illegal.'

'I'm not surprised,' he says. 'He was employing people who shouldn't have been working and he was paying no taxes.'

I'm certainly not naïve, but it had never occurred to me.

'So what's the worst that can happen?' I ask.

'Guess they'll close down the schools.'

'What about the money we're owed?' Nicolas was not good at paying the wages on time, and often would not show up at a school to pay the teachers. Sometimes he would instruct the receptionist to pay us from the petty cash, but there was never enough money. Whichever school we went to, he was always at one of the other schools and *incommunicado*. If I hadn't actually seen him at my initial interview, I would have questioned his existence.

'I don't know about you, but I haven't been paid for four weeks,' groans Frankie.

'Four weeks? Why did you let it go on for so long?' I admonished him.

I insisted on being paid every two weeks, in cash, as arranged at my interview.

Frankie was right, the schools were closed down. Such is the influence of the *Guardia*. I would not see Stefano again.

Neither Frankie nor I are prepared to just let it go. Through various ways and means we find Ottomanelli's private address. It is in Cassino, hence the name of the school, about eighty kilometres south-east of Rome.

The next day we take the train from Termini to Cassino and locate Ottomanelli's house, an imposing Baroque style villa surrounded by high walls, with large iron entrance gates. We can only see the top of the house from the street. There is a *citofono* on the security gate. Frankie presses the button and a female voice answers:

'*Pronto, qui e?*'
'*E' in casa, Signor Ottomanelli?*' asks Frankie.
'*Non c'e,*' comes the reply.
'*Quando ritorno?*'
'*Non so,*' I don't know. The line goes dead.

'I don't believe her, let's hang around and see what happens,' Frankie says to me.

We cross the road and sit on a bench to wait. I feel like a spy on a stakeout. We've been there for about forty minutes when we see the gates sliding open. A sleek grey Jaguar car pulls off the road and glides into the courtyard through the open gates. It's Nicolas.

Racing across the road we squeeze through the automatic gates before they slam shut. Nicolas gets out of his car looking startled, but when he recognises us, swaggers towards us smiling. He invites us into his house. It's sumptuous. Italian marble tiled floors covered with Persian rugs, and works of art adorn the walls, which must have cost a small fortune. Chandeliers in Murano glass cascade from the ceilings. The *Guardia* certainly hasn't seized any of his personal assets, I think to myself.

'Mr Ottomanelli,' begins Frankie.

He is cut off by Nicolas. 'First, let me say how sorry I am about your jobs, secondly you will be paid what you are owed.'

This takes the wind completely out of our sails as we were expecting a fight on our hands.

'Wait just a moment.' He leaves the room and we look at each other.

'What if he's calling his heavy boys to remove us, Frankie?' I mutter nervously.

The next minute Nicolas is back with fistfuls of money, which he proceeds to count out into two piles. He then hands one to me, and the other to Frankie.

'I think you will find it correct. *Buona sera.*' We're dismissed.

Outside, we both breathe a sigh of relief. Although it had been comparatively easy to get our money, we both knew that we had taken a big risk turning up on his doorstep.

Later that month, *'Il Corriere'* runs an article on tax evasion and misappropriation of funds by businesses associated with the Mafia. Although our school isn't mentioned we think it *is* rather a coincidence!

So now I need to find another teaching position. My private teaching is proving very lucrative and I have more than enough students. However, it's not a secure, regular income, as the students can cancel at any time.

Chris has a friend who runs a school in the Vatican City. It is affiliated to the church, and many of the young male students are training for the priesthood.

After submitting my CV, which I have updated on Chris's computer, I am offered a position to teach in the evenings, which I accept. The remuneration is slightly more than at my previous school, so I will be better off.

I thought I would be quite nervous about teaching novice priests, but in fact they are very good students and surprisingly worldly. I become very friendly with two of them in particular.

Petr is from Poland and extremely good looking. What a waste, I think to myself. He is a sculptor, and one day he brings one of his statues to class. His work is beautiful, but I fear that the full potential of his talent will not be realised, due to his chosen vocation.

Stefano is Italian. His older brother has disappointed the family by going into engineering and not the priesthood, so

Stefano is the family's last hope. I feel that he is not good material for the priesthood, but not wanting to upset his parents has allowed himself to be coerced into it. He is so well-mannered and compassionate. I think he would make a wonderful husband and father.

The student priests live in the Vatican Institute, Agostiniai Collegio S. Monica, and one day Petr and Stefano invite me to the institution.

The entrance to the college is hidden away in a corner of the Via del S. Uffizio. A small wrought-iron gate set in a large stone wall leads into a secluded garden, with little winding pathways between trees, shrubs and flowers. The building is an old stone monastery and the priests' cells are small but well furnished.

Petr, Stefano and I climb a stone staircase, which leads out onto the roof of the building. We are behind the larger than life-size statues that are atop St Peter's Basilica. The view from here is incredible.

Through Frederico, the Principal of the school, I am offered the chance to give private tutoring. One of my students is an ordained priest, Padre Lino. He lives in one of the Vatican colleges.

The lesson is from 3 pm. until 5 pm. When I arrive, I ring the bell on the gate. After a few minutes the Priest, dressed in long black robes, appears at the gate and lets me into a cloistered garden. He escorts me along cool, dark corridors with shiny red tiled floors that smell of polish, and we enter a large room, which contains a grand piano and lots of antique furniture. We sit opposite each other at a large desk. Halfway through the lesson a Filipino man brings us tea. It's so quiet you can hear a pin drop. I never see any other priests.

After the lesson, Padre Lino escorts me out of the building, through the cloisters, to the gate.

The Vatican City is the smallest independent state in the world. It is not part of the Papal States. It has its own government and rule of law, its own flag and anthem, its own automobile licence plates, and its own coins and postage stamps. The Italian postal service leaves a lot to be desired, but send a card from the Vatican post office and it will not only have its own Vatican City stamp, it is guaranteed to arrive promptly at its destination!

Walking through the Vatican one day on my way to school, I see a small crowd gathered at the gates of the Vatican gardens.

'Il Papa,' one of the onlookers says excitedly to me. *'Il Papa viene,'* the Pope is coming.

I am not a religious person, but I do love to go inside churches to see the architecture, statues and paintings, and I sometimes even light a candle and give a donation. Despite my lack of faith, the opportunity that presented itself to me at that moment was too good to ignore.

So I wait with the growing crowd until eventually our patience is rewarded. The automatic gates, manned by the Swiss Guard in their orange, red and black outfits, slide open and out glides a long black limousine.

The windows are tinted, but the Pope has opened his window so that we can see him. There is no mistaking the beatific face of the man sitting in the back of the car. As the car slides past me I am only meters away from him.

Although he is smiling and waving at the crowd, it is not hard to see that this is a sick man.

I feel privileged to have seen Pope John Paul II that day.

Maybe I am not being fair to Chris, and also not being fair to myself. Although I enjoy his company and value his friendship, I'm not romantically involved with him.

Over dinner at his place one evening, we have a heart to heart talk about our feelings for each other and agree to be just good friends. He confides in me that he's very attracted to dark Latino women.

I don't fit that descriptions at all, but I know just the woman who does!

I have befriended one of the other teachers at my new school. Anna Maria is a dark-haired beauty of Spanish parents. She speaks perfect Italian and is often mistaken for an Italian, on account of her long dark hair and Latino looks. Ani came to

Rome from Canada a couple of years ago. Although some years younger than Chris, I think they will get on very well.

Chris comes to the school one evening to pick me up. I ask him if he would mind giving Ani a lift home too, as I've heard there is a *sciopero*.

When I introduce them, I can see immediately that they are attracted to each other. Ani lives out of the city, so I ask Chris to drop me off at my apartment first.

The following evening when I see Ani after school, she tells me that she really likes Chris, and asks me how serious we are, as she is interested in seeing him again. He has also suggested as much to her.

'Would you mind?' she asks.

'Of course I don't mind, why should I?' In fact I feel really happy about it as it will give me more time to concentrate on Alessandro!

Daylight Robbery

My bedroom is my sanctuary. Although the smallest bedroom in the apartment, I feel it is the most comfortable. Originally the study, bookcases cover two of the walls. They are full of oversize books, mainly on art, and I spend many hours reading them.

I pull out the volume on my favourite Renaissance painter, Botticelli, and find a two-page colour plate of *The Birth of Venus*. I place some lira notes between the pages. This becomes my safe, as I do not have a bank account.

Since coming to Rome I've only been into a bank on one occasion. When I moved into my new apartment I needed to draw cash on my credit card. At home the doors of the banks stand wide open, but here the entrances have security cabins with double doors, which allow the entrance of only one person at a time. I needed to press a button to open the outer glass door, step into a cylindrical cubicle and wait for the door to close behind me, before the inner glass door opened automatically to let me into the bank. Momentarily locked into the glass cubicle I felt like a 'Trekkie' waiting for Scotty to 'beam me up'.

I am impressed at some of the security measures implemented in Rome. Shop frontages are shuttered when closed. Most apartment buildings have doormen, *palazzi* and villas are surrounded by high fences with security systems on the gates, and apartment doors can be locked by turning the key up to five times. The key operates a steel rod on the inside of the door which penetrates further into the floor with each turn of the key.

I am therefore puzzled when one day I arrive home from school and the front door is ajar. I push it open and find our landlady,

Signora De Luca and Allison talking to two *Carabinieri*. One of them is Allison's boyfriend, Andrea. They look very dashing in their navy uniform with a red stripe down the trousers, peaked cap and white gun holster. Allison is extremely upset.

'We've been burgled,' she sobs.

Allison's room has been ransacked and money, along with some jewellery and her camera, has been stolen.

I rush to my room which doesn't appear to have been touched, and open the dresser drawer where I keep a small amount of cash and my valuables. Some of my favourite jewellery has gone. A gold neck chain from an erstwhile boyfriend, a gold chain bracelet with a charm of Nefertiti, which was a birthday present, a gold ring with a black opal stone which I bought in Australia and another ring with a topaz stone that I'd had for many years. Apart from the monetary value, they were of immense sentimental value and irreplaceable.

Surprisingly, the cash which I'd tucked away in the back of the drawer is still there.

I turn to the bookcase and pull out the Botticelli book. Of course, the money is still there. I thank my lucky stars, and Sandro.

Andrea tells me that a neighbour had noticed someone acting suspiciously on the landing outside the apartment door, and had called the police. When they arrived there was no-one on the landing, but there was someone inside the flat.

The neighbour had also contacted Signora De Luca to come and open the apartment door. Hiding inside were two gypsy children, who were taken to the local police station. Allison had arrived home shortly afterwards.

According to the police, the children were pushed through a very small window situated on the landing at the top of the stairs, onto our kitchen balcony, probably by an older sibling or a parent, and had gained entry to the apartment through the kitchen window. The children went through the apartment stealing small items and then threw them out of a window to a second accomplice waiting below in the street. The kids would then have been pulled back through their access window by the first accomplice waiting on the landing, since the front door, having been triple-locked, could not have been opened from the inside for the children to make an exit.

Both accomplices however, had run off when they heard the police sirens, leaving the children to their own devices, knowing that the police can do nothing to the children because they are underage.

After questioning the children the police get no information from them and eventually have to let them go.

Eileen always locks her bedroom door when she goes out. The lock hasn't been broken. When she arrives home later she checks her room and everything is in place. I think she was the lucky one. They obviously didn't get around to her room. In fact, the police think they had disturbed the kids while they were in my room. Eileen had a considerable amount of cash in a drawer.

The next day she goes to the Via dei Condotti and blows it in Dolce & Gabbana!

Eileen tells me she is going to see a clairvoyant.

'Don't suppose I can come along?' I ask. I've only been to a clairvoyant once before and feel I need a reading. Maybe she can tell me whether I'm going to get laid or not.

Maria lives in Trastevere, a middle-aged lady who inherited the 'gift' from her mother and grandmother. She only speaks Italian, so in order not to lose anything in translation, we invite Ani to come along to interpret and take notes.

Eileen has her reading first and then it's my turn. When I walk into Maria's consulting room, I feel that I have entered another galaxy. Rich, bright fabrics with zodiac signs are draped around the room. Framed prints of gods, goddesses and deities cover the walls. In the centre of the room stands a little round table. I fully expect to see Maria in gypsy costume, complete with gold coined headscarf and crystal ball.

I must 'cross her palm' with 20,000 lire before we begin the reading. She reads the tarot cards.

First, she asks me to cut the pack of cards and then she reads the name on the uppermost card.

'*Cybele*. You have chosen the best card. The Prophetess. One of the great oracles of antiquity. In classical mythology she is the Goddess of knowledge who presided over the destinies of men.'

She continues. 'You live life intensely with sensitivity, intelligently.'

Maria then deals more cards and reads them.

'You have never followed a single path. You have almost lived two different lives running parallel. Destiny is guiding your path straight but it is difficult to follow because you present your own obstacles.'

This, I think, is quite true. My life has never been simple or straightforward.

'You are influenced by a love relationship in the past. This relationship is still influencing you today. It is separate but still part of your life. An incident in the past caused your path to transform around the age of twenty.'

Right again. I did have a traumatic relationship at the age of twenty-one, which had profound consequences on my future.

'Fortunately you are a person of many desires. Thanks to your Will and ability you will again find the straight path. Abandon your dreams. It is your dreams which are impeding you, let them go. There is a person who is very interested in you. There is a young man who creates confusion in your path. He's very attached to you. He finds balance with you. He's a great seducer. Don't follow him, let him go. The future is good. There is a situation now which is confused, painful, but will be resolved by your strong Will. The cards are very favourable. Fate will help you. Destiny will bring new things.'

'Will I ever find the man of my dreams?' I ask her.

'You have already met him. There is a man who you already know, and he will be the great love of your life. It is within your ability to ensure the relationship goes well.'

'Can you give me more information?' I venture.

'No,' she shakes her head.

So, is it someone who is in my life at the moment? Is it Frankie, Alessandro?

'There is a person who is very interested in you but the interest is physical.'

Don't think that can be Frankie, but maybe Alessandro? Hardly!

'There is a young man who creates confusion in your path.'

Who is this creator of confusion?

She then takes my hand and reads my palm.

'You live life as if you had three different lives. You've never been able to live one way. So much so, that life has always been confused and you have not followed the single path.'

Three lives now? Well, I do have three jobs!

'You are very intelligent and can succeed and have what you want. You never felt the same as your family even as a child. You always followed your own path.'

True, my mother always used to say I was 'odd'.

'You have a dream which will be realised.'

She then tells me that she can answer three questions, but I should think them in my head. When I am ready for the answer I should nod. They must be questions that only require a 'yes' or 'no' answer.

I close my eyes and think of the first question.

Is the man of my dreams in my life now? I nod that I am ready for her answer. She turns over a card.

'Yes,' she answers.

Is he here in Rome? I think the second question and nod. She turns over another card.

'Yes.'

I have one more question.

Is it Frankie or Alessandro? I think the last question and nod. She turns over the last card

'Yes.'

Too late I realise my blunder. That was the end of the session. I leave, still none the wiser about who the man of my dreams could be!

Frankie has won a green card in a lottery. He was so desperate to get to the United States of America that he paid a lawyer US

$2,000 to enter him into the lottery. Every year, fifty-thousand places are available from countries around the world.

He couldn't believe his luck when he found out he'd been successful and I'll never forget the day he told me.

I'm on my way home from Piazza Bologna one evening when my mobile rings.

'*Pronto* Frankie,' I respond when I see his name appear on the screen.

'*Ciao,* Margarita.' He sounds very excited. 'Great news, I've won a green card in the lottery.'

I swallow hard. I know it means a lot to him and I'm happy for him, but I also know what is bound to happen.

'Congratulations.'

'I should be able to go in about three months,' he was saying, 'after all my documentation has been finalised.'

'Three months!' I exclaim, trying not to sound too disappointed. 'That's great.' I can't let him hear how upset I really am.

First Gayle, then Eugene and now Frankie would be leaving Rome.

The Churches of Rome

People say that once you've seen one church, you've seen them all. Not true. Well not in Rome anyway. The churches in Rome are all unique and well worth a visit—but there are over 900 of them!

I would love to take certain of my boyfriends, past and present, to the pretty little Byzantine church called Santa Maria in Cosmedin. There, I would ask them to put their hand into the *Bocca della Verita*, The Mouth of Truth. If they have been lying to me the sculpture will bite off their hand! The sculpture is mounted on a wall outside the church. It is thought to be an ancient manhole cover portraying the face of a river god—probably Oceanus—with an open mouth. It's quite entertaining to stand and watch the crowd of people lining up to put their hand inside the mouth, and comical to see how reluctant some of them are to do it!

In the film *Roman Holiday* when Audrey Hepburn and Gregory Peck visit The Mouth of Truth, Peck challenges Hepburn to place her hand inside the mouth, which she does. She then asks Peck to do the same thing. Peck puts in his hand. He has pulled his sleeve over his hand when Hepburn isn't looking, so when he removes it from the mouth it appears his hand has been bitten off. Hepburn freaks out until she realises it's just a prank!

A little way along the Via Veneto is another church with a surprise. It is called Santa Maria della Concezione dei Cappuccini, commonly known as 'The Church of the Bones'.

About halfway up the stairs to the church there is an entrance that leads into the ossuary of the Capuchin friars. When one of the friars dies he is buried in a vault, and after some time the bones are removed and placed in this ossuary, which holds the bones of more than four thousand friars. There are several chambers and the bones are arranged into intricate patterns over the walls, roof and floor of these chambers.

Call it spooky, unhealthy or downright macabre, but it really is a fascinating sight and one not to be missed.

Another church, and perhaps one of my favourites, is the Church of S.S. Nero e Achilleo. I find it by accident.

One warm sunny day, after having lunch with Dawn at La FAO, I am enjoying a walk along the Via Delle Terme di Caracalla. The road is lined with pine trees, and as I walk on the carpet of fallen pine needles, they crack under my shoes and release a pleasing fragrance.

I spot the building hidden amongst the trees and decide to go and investigate. The façade is very plain, and because the church is set back from the road, hidden amongst the pine trees, it could easily be missed. At first I think it has been left to go to ruin, but when I push on the old oak door it creaks open.

Stepping inside I feel immediately chilled. It is so cold, but the lights are on and a couple of candles are lit on the *Offerte* box. I walk slowly around the church looking at the frescoes on the walls. I recoil. Although beautifully painted, the content is quite horrific. I hear a step behind me and, startled, I turn around to face an old bent man. He must be all of a hundred years old. Quasimodo! Wait, isn't he in the wrong church? He tells me he is the curator. He talks in rapid Italian and I catch about every other word.

He explains that the church is fourth-century and is one of the original titular churches of Rome. Nereus and Achilleus, to whom the church is dedicated, were soldiers and martyrs. The frescoes on the walls, he explains, depict the martyrdom of the Saints and Apostles. Not for the faint-hearted, these frescoes are explicit in the execution of the Saints. Some were boiled alive, stoned to death, dismembered, decapitated, skinned alive, crucified, stabbed, beaten, and hung drawn and quartered! Absolutely gruesome, but fascinating.

Then Quasimodo asks me to follow him, and leads me into

the back of the church to a large chapel. We stand on a glass panel and look below into the excavations. This is the original part of the foundations, dating back to the fourth-century.

Walking back into the church I notice the pews are covered in green satin with large bouquets of white roses placed at the end of the pews. There are many bouquets all around the church. Surprisingly, despite the horrific images, this church is a popular venue for wedding ceremonies. Quasimodo tells me that one is taking place later that afternoon at four o'clock.

I decide to walk for a while and when I return later a small group is gathered outside the church. The doors are closed and locked. All in the group, both men and women, are dressed in black. I wonder if I have misunderstood and it's a funeral, then I hear the word *matrimonio,* which means marriage. I strike up a conversation with one of the guests who assures me, '*Si, certo*' there will be a wedding at four o'clock. More guests start to arrive and everyone is getting agitated because the doors are still closed. Eventually the Priest arrives and the relief is palpable.

A few minutes later the bride arrives looking radiant in a cream satin dress. She carries a bouquet of white lilies and roses. She wears a short veil, fastened by a mother-of pearl comb, which her husband-to-be removes from her face at the altar. They kiss on both cheeks. Two small stools with red velvet seats are placed behind them to sit on and the ceremony begins.

The Saints, their mouths agape and hands outstretched, as if pleading for help, look down upon the couple who stand before the altar solemnly taking their marriage vows and, like the rest of the congregation, seem blissfully unaware of the horrific images that encompass them. Bizarre!

After the ceremony the Priest moves around the church to give his blessing. It's time to make my exit.

Quasimodo is standing at the entrance to the church. He follows me outside into the warm evening sun. I'm beginning to feel like Esmeralda!

This old man seems to have taken quite a shine to me. Maybe all the wedding ceremonies that have been performed here have got to him, because he tells me he is looking for a wife and would I be interested? Of course, I don't want to hurt his feelings as he seems pretty serious, and I refuse politely. At least I've had a proposal in Rome!

Like many Italians, Luana and Gianni have a house at the beach. Theirs is in the province of Latino in a village called Borgo Grappa.

They invite me to stay with them for the long weekend in May. I'm happy to accept as I feel exhausted with my daily routine.

We drive the seventy-two kilometres south from Rome, passing through Nettuno, a modern town with wide sandy beaches on the Tyrhhenian Sea, Lavinio, another small beachside town, and San Felice Cercio, until we arrive at the small seaside town of Borgo Grappa.

Set in a quiet location amidst gardens full of bougainvilleas, the apartment is small, but adequate for a holiday home. From the terrace on the top floor the sea is visible in the distance. Luana has chosen green, yellow and blue for the décor, which looks very bright and cheerful and blends in well with the surroundings, echoing the colours of the garden and the seascape beyond.

The following morning we cycle the two kilometres to the beach. It's many years since I've ridden a bike, but after a few initial wobbles I get my balance and try to catch up with Luana, who seems to be in training for the *Tour de France*!

Arriving at the beach, we leave our bikes on the side of the road, clamber over the sand dunes, and find a fairly secluded spot to soak up the sun.

By noon it's getting a little too hot for me and there is very little shade. Luana, whose skin is already the colour of mahogany, is basking in the sun. I don't want to end up the colour of a lobster again, so we cycle back home to have lunch with Gianni.

In the evening we drive to nearby Sabaudia, a jet-set playground, set in the middle of a National Park with grazing buffalo, which is renowned for its *mozzarella* and excellent food. We eat swordfish at a restaurant on the beach and watch the sunset over the sea.

There are lots of festivities in the town and in the local park people are dancing to a small group of musicians. Both Luana and Gianni are avid dancers, as I am, so we pass away a couple of hours tripping the light fantastic, until the band packs up and everyone leaves at midnight.

On our last morning, Luana and I visit the fish market at the harbour in nearby San Felice Circeo. A fisherman walks between the market stalls, a huge swordfish slung over his shoulder. Its dead eyes are wide open and staring right at me. I feel sorry for it, but I probably ate some of his brother last night! We buy fresh giant sized prawns for lunch and after the obligatory *siesta* head back to Rome.

During the summer, I make several trips to other nearby towns with Luana and Gianni. The areas immediately outside of Rome are well worth a visit, but surprisingly neglected by tourists.

We visit two of the most attractive hilltop towns; Rocca di Pappa, which is an enchanting tangle of narrow streets and old churches, and Grottaferrata facing the Alban Lakes about twenty-five kilometres south-east of Rome.

We stop the car high on a ridge above Lake Albano. The views of the lake, the woods in the distance and the Palace of Castel Gandolfo on the opposite mountain are superb.

Another weekend we head east to Tivoli, a historic hill town in the Lazio Region, about an hour's drive from Rome on the Via Tiburtina.

We spend the day visiting two of the main attractions; the extensive ruins of Hadrian's Villa, with a gigantic complex of lakes, fountains, libraries, baths, temples and gardens, and the magnificent renaissance Villa d'Este, which has breathtaking gardens, composed mainly of water fountains. There are fountains of every description. The centrepiece is the gigantic Water Organ Fountain which cascades down a huge drop into a quiet shady pool.

Looking for Shoes

'I did not have three thousand pairs of shoes. I had one thousand and sixty' Imelda Marcos said.

Being a shoe addict, I am in my element in Rome and spend many happy hours looking for shoes.

In my wardrobe at home I have stacks of boxes containing shoes, all arranged in colour order, height of heel, casual, smart, or what I call taxi shoes—shoes that can only be worn from the house to the taxi, from the taxi to the restaurant and vice-versa— because the heels are too high for everyday wear. I have photographs pasted on the end of each box, so I can see at a glance which pair of shoes is inside.

Rome has three main department stores, Standa, Coin and Rinascente. Most shops are individual boutique style shops and along the Via Nazionale there are numerous shoe shops.

On my way to visit Dawn one Saturday afternoon, I have a very interesting experience.

I'm walking along the Via Nazionale when a very stylish, but sensible pair of Valleverde shoes in the window of Peppy, attract my attention. I need some smart black shoes for work, so I enter the shop and a young, handsome sales assistant approaches me.

'*Buongiorno Signorina,*' he greets me with the flattering title of *Signorina*, usually reserved for younger women. I think Italians do it intentionally to throw you off guard.

In Rome all shoes are displayed in the window and it is normal practice to point out to the sales assistant the desired shoe in the window, which I do.

'*Trenta nove,*' I answer when he asks my size.

He ushers me to a seat at the back of the shop and disappears behind a screen into the storeroom. After a few minutes, he reappears with two pairs of shoes. One is the style I asked for, but the other is a completely different style with a higher heel.

Sitting on the low footstool in front of me, he helps me into the first pair, which is too tight. Then he suggests I try on the other pair.

'But they are not what I want,' I complain, resorting to English.

He is not going to take no for an answer and is removing the shoes from the box. Oh well, no harm in trying them on.

'*Che carina,*' he smiles when I have them on.

Although I have long since mastered the art of walking in high heels on Rome's cobblestones, I stick to my guns.

'These are too high,' I protest, teetering precariously on the spiky heels.

'Please, I have some more for you,' and with that he disappears again behind the screen into the back of the shop.

He seems to be taking too long, and I am just considering walking out when he reappears, carrying another box with Manolo Blahnik printed on it.

Nestling in the tissue paper is a pair of shoes with perilously high heels. I open my mouth to protest again, but then quickly close it when he removes them from the box. They are very flimsy with just two thin straps over the toes and an ankle strap. The heels are high enough to induce vertigo. They're gorgeous.

'Taxi shoes,' I think to myself. Although I'm looking for some sensible shoes for work and my patience is wearing thin, I can't resist in trying them on.

This time he sits astride the footstool while he is helping me into the shoes, making sure that my foot is against his crotch. He caresses my ankle as he fastens the buckle and then runs his hands up and down my leg from my ankle to mid-calf. Jeeez! He's getting off on this!

'*Bella,*' he smiles.

I look around the shop but no one seems to have noticed my dilemma. All the sales assistants are busy with other customers.

'*Basta,*' enough, I say, and promptly make to take off the

shoes, whereupon he jumps up and goes behind the screen again. I struggle to undo the ankle straps, aware that he is in my line of vision and is watching me. He is making 'pssst pssst' noises, trying to attract my attention. When I glance up he is making lewd gestures.

It's the last image I have of him as I flee from the shop!

The Love Bunnies

One scorching hot day in July, Chris, Ani and I head out of Rome in Chris's convertible towards Florence. We skirt around Florence and head up into the hills to Fiesole, where we will be staying at the Villa San Girolomo, a convent run by an order of Irish Carmelite nuns who open their doors as a *pensione* to visitors in the summer. Chris manoeuvres the car up the winding road, past the Piazza Garibaldi and into Piazza Mina, the main square where I met Flavia over two years ago.

We turn left down the narrow Via Fiesolana and stop at a large grey wrought-iron gate. Chris climbs out of the car and rings the cow bell that hangs on the wall by the gate. A nun wearing a grey habit, with a starched white wimple covering her head and a large crucifix around her neck, hurries to open the gates. We drive into a pebbled courtyard that has a well in the centre and pull up in front of the convent.

The small reception area is dominated by a large painting of the Crucifixion. I don't recognise the artist, but I'm sure it's an original by an Italian Master.

We check into our rooms, which, like most convent accommodation, are clean but austere and sparsely furnished, with just a small wardrobe, a chair and a writing table. A crucifix hangs on the wall over the single bed. There is no mirror.

The room is dark and cool. I open the windows and the shutters, and catch my breath. Below me are the rolling hills of Tuscany and in the distance, nestling amidst the lush green countryside of ubiquitous pines, cypress and silver green olive trees, is Florence, Il Duomo, with its terracotta cupola, visible in the distance. I drink in the evocative panorama.

After we've freshened up, we walk back to Piazza Mina

and have lunch on the terrace at Villa Aurora, which also has panoramic views of the landscape. We linger over lunch and then walk slowly back to the convent for a *siesta*.

In the evening after a light meal, Ani and I stroll through the gardens of the convent. She confides in me that Chris has asked her to marry him.

The previous weekend they had driven to Verona in the north of Italy to visit the thirteenth-century home of the Cappello family who, according to legend were the Capulets of Shakespeare's play, *Romeo and Juliet*.

On the legendary balcony Chris had asked Ani to marry him.

'How romantic', I reply. 'Did you accept?'

She hesitates. 'I said I needed more time. I feel everything is moving too fast. He wants my answer before we go back to Rome.'

Before we leave the convent, one of the sisters tries to recruit me as a nun. Apparently the number of younger women taking up the calling is declining, so as the older nuns die off, there will be a shortage of nuns. It would certainly fulfil the desire I once had of living in the hills above Florence. But I couldn't sign up for a life of celibacy!

The following day after breakfast, we head off to Orvieto, a medieval hilltop town in Umbria. On arrival, we park the car and walk to the main square. We sit on the steps of the Cathedral and observe the locals.

Later, Chris and Ani move away to a quiet spot to meditate. I watch the children playing in the piazza. Old men, their faces brown and leathery, sit around drinking strong black coffee, while women gather in small groups to have a chat, *chiacchierare*. Young lovers stroll hand in hand. It's so peaceful and there is a strong community feel about the place. Everyone seems to know each other, and from time to time greet each other with *'Ciao, come stai?'*

Just before we set off for Rome, Ani announces that she has accepted Chris's proposal of marriage.

Ani and Chris become inseparable and she eventually moves into his apartment in Monte Verdi Vecchio.

Two little toy rabbits, one pink and one blue, which they had bought from a little toy shop in Orvieto, sit together in their bedroom, arms entwined.

The Eternal City

I never cease to be in awe of this atmospheric city with its abundance of culture and history. The Romans seem so blasé about it.

On the way to school, I stare out of the window of the number 90 bus and never tire of looking at the ancient monuments. It's like living in a museum and I have to pinch myself to believe I am really here, living the dream, in the Eternal City.

'Io Sono Italiana.' I'm Italian, I'd say if someone asked me, *'Da dove sei?'* 'Where are you from?'

Of course, it's quite obvious that I'm not Italian, but I really feel rooted here with a strong sense of belonging. I'm in a permanent state of euphoria. Rome seems to have a positive psychological effect on my state of wellbeing. Maybe my ancestors had been Italian. When Julius Caesar invaded Britain nearly 2000 years ago, maybe a Roman soldier had seduced a Celtic woman, and I am a descendent of that liaison? Or perhaps by some strange quirk of fate, my Italian soul has entered an English body. Hence, my yearning for all things Italian.

Suffice to say, sometimes I feel more Italian than English. In fact many people tell me that I am too passionate to be English.

'Are you sure you're English and not Italian?' Alessandro asks me with his crooked smile.

I take it as a compliment, as I do when people stop me in the street and ask for directions in Italian. I must look like one of the locals.

I recently read a quote by Nathanial Hawthorne, a tourist in Rome, who found himself gradually turning into an expatriate. I think it sums up my feelings at the moment:

'The years after all have a kind of emptiness, when we spend too many of them on a foreign shore. We defer the reality of life, in such cases, until a future moment, when we shall again breathe our native air, but, by and by, there are no future moments, or if we do return, we find that the native air has lost its invigorating quality, and that life has shifted in reality to the spot where we have deemed ourselves only temporary residents. Thus, between two countries we have none at all, or only that little space of either in which we finally lay down our discontented bones'.

The phone rings.

'Pronto.'

'Ciao bella.' It's Frankie's voice.

My heart always skips a beat when I hear his voice, and this time is no exception. I have no idea that this phone call will change my life's direction once again.

'I need to talk to you,' he says.

'Okay, go ahead.'

'No, no, not over the phone, I need to see you.'

There is something in his voice, something I cannot quite put my finger on, a sense of urgency.

'Is something wrong?'

'No, not really. Just come and meet me if you can at Campo de' Fiori in about an hour.'

'I'll meet you in the wine bar,' I suggest.

I'm trembling as I put down the telephone. What can possibly have happened? He didn't sound upset. In fact he sounded very excited. Perhaps it's good news about some acting work. He's been to lots of auditions lately.

I take the bus to Campo de' Fiori to the little wine bar where Frankie and I often meet. Hundreds of dusty wine bottles line the walls and ceiling. The floor is wooden and covered in sawdust, which reminds me of some of the old pubs in England.

Frankie is already sitting at one of the little tables in the corner. Massive Attack is playing on the CD player:

'Karmacoma, Jamaica aroma…'

He stands to greet me, kisses me the very friendly Italian way of two kisses on each cheek. '*Ciao cara.*'

He orders a bottle of my favourite red wine and pours two glasses.

'Is everything okay?' I ask.

Frankie takes my hand and looks intently into my eyes. His eyes are green like mine. He looks very serious.

'I've had an offer of work,' he says excitedly, 'for a lead role in a play that will run for at least six months.'

I breathe a sigh of relief. 'That's terrific news,' I answer. 'I'm so happy for you, tell me about it.'

He takes a deep breath.

'Well,' he says toying with his glass.

Warning bells are ringing in my head. Why is he stalling?

'Karmacoma, Jamaica aroma…'

'Well,' he says again, 'it's for a theatre company based in America, so if I accept the part I'll be going to New York.'

'New York!' I exclaim. I'm gobsmacked. Then as it slowly sinks in I ask him, 'and when will you be going?'

'It could be anytime, as soon as my visa is sorted out. I'm waiting to hear from them.'

So, I thought, it's been on the cards for a while.

'That's wonderful.' I manage to say. 'Congratulations.'

We lapse into silence.

'Look,' he says, his eyes penetrating mine, 'I have a proposition to put to you.'

I don't say a word. I just look at him, as the tears start to well up in my eyes.

'Why don't you come with me? We could find an apartment together.'

'You sure you want to be with me I've nothing to give Karmacoma, Jamaica aroma…'

'What do you mean,' I ask. 'As friends?'

He sighs and squeezes my hand tightly.

'Look, I don't know what may happen, I love you but I can't make any promises. I'm making a serious commitment in all ways except one. Don't come with a hidden agenda of trying to convert me. Just think about it.'

'Walking through the suburbs though not exactly lovers you're a couple, Karmacoma, Jamaica aroma...'

'I will,' I promise.

'Karmacoma, Jamaica aroma.'

We finish our drinks as Massive Attack finish their song and we step out into the cool night air. I shiver involuntarily, and Frankie puts his arm around me.

We walk together into the piazza. The night sky is full of stars that appear as diamonds sewn onto a black velvet cloth. The moon is full. I feel that we are coming to the end of an era and from this moment on things will never be the same. Without Frankie everything will change.

We carry on walking along the Fiori Imperiale until we reach the Colosseum. I remember the first time I saw the ancient monument with Gayle when I first arrived in Rome, nearly two years ago.

When we reach my apartment, I kiss him and hurriedly go inside, so that he doesn't see the tears in my eyes. I feel I am losing my best friend.

'Think about it,' he'd said. And I did. All night.

It's raining at last. I'm woken-up by the pitter-patter of raindrops on the window pane. It steadily gets heavier.

I slip out of bed and throw open the window and the shutters. The heavens have opened. It's bucketing down. *Piove a catinelle,* raining cats and dogs! The streets are awash. The traffic doesn't slow down, and as each car passes, a wall of water rises like a mini tsunami and washes over the pavements. Irate pedestrians swear at the passing vehicles as they paddle through the backwash.

'Vaffanculo!' I hear one *bella donna* shout, after a car has soaked her.

The fresh smell of rain permeates through my apartment. I love the smell. It will lay the dust, wash the streets, and cool down the ancient stones of the city, which retain their heat like oven bricks.

Tempers will subside. I have noticed in a hot climate, people become irritable. After a hot spell, rain is like a cold shower and cools people down.

I dress quickly and leave the apartment, grabbing my *impermeabile,* raincoat. The rain has slowed to a steady pace. It feels good on my face.

Allison always takes her umbrella. She wants to make sure that the first few drops of rain fall on her umbrella and not on her body.

'Acid rain,' she explains to me. 'The first few drops are acid rain.'

I walk down to the nearby piazza. The fountain is flowing. So much water everywhere! The cobblestones gleam, polished by the rain.

Slowly I walk back up the hill, and by the time I reach my apartment the rain has almost stopped. I step out onto my terrace. Below I hear the steady swish of tyres on the wet road. There is a slit of light in the clouds. Soon the sun will emerge and steam will rise from the ground.

I lift up my head and let the last few drops of rain trickle down my face and prepare for more hot weather.

Arrivederci Roma

> Its image is so great
> That it cannot be kept in the soul.
> GOETHE

I wake up one day and know it's time to leave. Burnout has set in after nearly two years!

I am still confused about my feelings towards Frankie and have kept in contact with him, sometimes talking on the telephone for hours. He is still asking me to join him in New York and it seems more and more attractive after each conversation. The night before he left Rome, he reminded me of his offer and said that he meant every word. I really miss him. More importantly, I'm gradually coming to terms with the fact that our relationship will never be consummated.

My relationship with Alessandro doesn't seem to be going anywhere. It's still exciting and romantic, but we seem to be in a rut, and as my ex-boss used to say 'a rut is a shallow grave'. I feel that we are drifting aimlessly, and that he is quite content to let the situation carry on as it is, without making a commitment. The anticipation and exhilaration that I feel before we meet always ends in disappointment and frustration. I'll never get the opportunity to act out my fantasies!

I feel that I'm being pulled in two different directions. 'You have never followed a single path' Maria, the clairvoyant, had said; but she had also said 'There's a man in your life causing confusion, don't follow him, let him go.'

Eventually, after much soul-searching and many sleepless

nights, I reach a decision to go to New York for three months. If it doesn't work out at least I will have tried, and I can always come back to Rome.

I make the telephone call one evening to Frankie. This is it.

The phone rings several times, and I expect the answering machine to pick up, when his voice comes on the line, a little drowsy. It is early morning in New York.

'Hi Frankie, I've got some news for you.' I never need to say it's me.

'When are you coming?' he asks.

How does he know me so well!

He's absolutely over the moon, and I feel reassured that I've made the right decision.

I telephone my landlady and arrange to see her the following afternoon, at her apartment in San Giovanni in Laterano, a stone's throw from the Colosseum. When I tell her that I'm leaving, she's really sad.

'You girls have been some of the best tenants I've had,' she sighs. She recounts some horror stories about several of her previous tenants.

It's true that Eileen, Allison and I had always respected and taken care of the apartment. We employed Signora De Luca's house cleaner once a week, and in the meantime cleaned it ourselves, so when Signora De Luca came to collect the rent the place always looked spick and span.

There had been one incident when Allison had invited her boyfriend for dinner, and had placed a hot tureen of soup directly onto the oak table. It had burnt a ring in the wood. We confessed to Signora De Luca immediately and hired a French polisher who made it look like new. I think she really respected us for telling her and making the repair.

Allison and Eileen are really disappointed that I'm leaving. They decide they would like to stay on in the apartment after I leave, and are quite happy to pay the rent between them. Signora De Luca is in agreement and the lease is passed over to Eileen.

I give notice to the school and also to my private students, who are all sorry that I'm leaving.

Then I have to break the news to all my friends, and, of course, Alessandro. That will be the hardest thing to do.

I decide not to tell him just yet. I want a few more nights with him before I do that. I don't want the dynamics of the relationship to change, which I think might happen as soon as I tell him. I'd like our relationship to continue growing, although I've given up on the idea of a sexual relationship. If it was going to happen, it would have happened by now. Just one night of passion before I left would have been great, but then wouldn't that become a one-night stand? And what if I'm disappointed in him as a lover? Maybe it's just better to dream of what might have been.

So, I continue to see him and enjoy his company, although inwardly I'm very sad.

It's as if he can sense that something is wrong. One night he asks me:

'*Cara*, what's the problem, you seem distant?'

I smile. 'Nothing wrong, just a little tired.'

I dread having to tell him that I'm leaving and toy with the idea of sending him a letter after I've gone, or maybe getting Franca to deliver a note to him in Piazza Navona. I try to imagine his face when he reads the letter and know I can't do that. He deserves more. No, I will have to tell him face to face.

But not tonight.

I start to pack. It's amazing how much I've accumulated during my two years in Rome. I fill one suitcase with books, another with shoes and handbags, and two others with clothes. I decide to send three of them to London by courier.

A week before I am due to leave I break the news to Alessandro. It isn't planned. I just find an opportune moment and probably that's what I've been waiting for. I've been procrastinating far too long.

It's Friday night and I stop at Piazza Navona as usual, after school, to see Alessandro. As we are walking to his lock-up container, I realise it's now or never. I wait until he's put away all his gear and suddenly blurt out: 'Alessandro, I've decided to leave Rome. I'll be going next week.'

He stops dead in his tracks and turns to me. 'I knew there was something.'

Then he puts his arms around me and kisses me hard and long. *'Andiamo,'* he says, and steers me towards his motorbike.

He doesn't ask me where I want to go. He just takes me home.

'I will see you again won't I?' I ask. My heart is thudding. Is this it?

'Yes, before you leave,' he murmurs. My eyes search his face. I can't read anything into his expression. Surely now would be the time for him to declare his undying love? Has he no feelings? He says nothing.

I let myself into the apartment, closing the door quietly behind me. Tip-toeing into my room, I fling myself across the bed and indulge in a good cry.

Is it possible to be in love with two men at the same time?

'All for the best,' my head is saying.

But my heart is saying something else.

My flatmates decide to give me a farewell bash. They will arrange it all. I just have to turn up. It's scheduled for the Friday night before I leave on the Saturday.

My last teaching day is Thursday and I take my students out for a pizza.

Friday arrives and I have neither seen nor heard from Alessandro. I feel sad and disappointed. I don't want to leave things in the air. I know he can't come to my party as he is working, but I am getting very anxious that time is running out and I may not see him at all before I leave.

I jump when my mobile phone rings. His name shows up on the screen.

'Ciao, Alessandro.'

'Ciao. Come'stai?' Just the sound of his voice sets my pulse racing.

'Bene, tu?'

'Abbastanza bene.'

He doesn't sound too good and I'm starting to have some

misgivings that I'm making the right move after all. Maybe he cares more than I think.

'*Ci vediamo stasera?*' he volunteers.

'Yes, I will see you this evening,' I say, 'after the party.'

My guests start to arrive around six o'clock. Susanna and Gianni arrive first with Marco and Monica, followed closely by Luana and Gianni, Ani and Chris, Franca, Dawn and Signora De Luca.

My flatmates have done me proud. The long oak table is full of appetizing food.

Susanna and Gianni give me a gift of a gold bracelet with a coin charm. Chris and Ani also give me a gold bracelet with a charm of Nefertiti's head, to replace the one that I'd had stolen.

Allison puts Jovanotti on the CD player that I bought from Eugene for 200,000 lire before he left, and that I have now sold to her for 100,000 lire. Jovanotti is a popular young Italian singer and songwriter with religious, political and philosophical messages in his lyrics.

It's an evening full of mixed emotions with some of the friends I've made in Rome, although some special friends are missing, Gayle, Frankie and Eugene and, of course, Alessandro. I can't wait to see him and keep sneaking glances at the clock.

Finally, around ten o'clock, the party breaks up and people start to leave. By eleven o'clock everyone has gone. Eileen and Allison refuse to let me help them clear up.

Pulling on my jacket, I leave the house and jump onto the first bus that comes along. It drops me at Largo Argentina outside La Feltrinella bookshop. From there I can easily walk along to Piazza Navona. It's now close to midnight and I quicken my pace. Supposing Alessandro has already gone? No, surely he'd call me. I take out my mobile phone and call him. He answers immediately.

'*Pronto Mar-ga-ret, dov'e sei?*'

'*Sto arrivando.*' I'm coming.

'*Ti sto aspettando.*' He's waiting for me.

I almost run the last fifty metres across the Piazza towards the lone figure of Alessandro. I fling my arms around him. He hugs and kisses me and we walk out of the Piazza together for the last time. I turn around to take one final look. The bars and restaurants have all closed for the night. It's deserted. I feel that I've been transported back in time, caught in a time warp in this ancient piazza.

The moon reflected in the water of the fountains casts an ethereal dancing light over the façades of the buildings, like one of those mirror balls in a dancehall. I catch my breath. I want to freeze this moment.

We call into a nearby bar for a drink. Some of the other artists are there with their girlfriends and we spend an hour or so with them. I'm getting impatient. I want him all to myself tonight. Finally we leave.

We set off on his motorbike and I cling to him tightly as we cross the Tiber and head up the hill to Gianicolo. Alessandro parks the bike in the piazza and we walk to the low stone wall which overlooks the city. There are lots of couples sitting on the wall. It's a popular place for lovers. We gaze down at the twinkling lights below us. Alessandro puts his arm around me, draws me towards him and whispers, *'Tu sei speciale.'*

I'm special. *Now* he tells me!

We talk into the wee small hours, and just as the sun comes up we head back down the hill, over the river and along a deserted Fiori Imperiale. The street cleaners have been around and the streets look clean and fresh. The tyres of Alessandro's bike make a swishing noise on the glistening, newly washed, roads.

As we skirt around the Colosseum the sun peeks through the arches, illuminating them, just as the spotlights had illuminated them on my first night in Rome.

I tighten my arms around Alessandro and we speed on until we reach my apartment.

At the door, we don't speak. We just hold each other tightly. He kisses me, tenderly at first and then hungrily.

I groan inwardly. Oh God, please don't do that or I'll change my mind. I have to go.

As if he can read my mind he says, 'You know if you change your mind you must come back. I will be here *come una lampada.'*

'*Arrivederci.*'

There. It's done. Without another word or backward glance he roars off on his motorbike, the drone of his engine getting fainter and fainter in the distance.

When I can no longer hear it I turn and enter the apartment. The sun has now come up fully and the stone façades of the buildings take on a terracotta hue.

I can hear the flow of early morning traffic and shouts of '*Buongiorno*' as the steel shutters of the shops are raised.

It's a new day in Rome, but I will not be a part of it.

* * *

So, here I am about to board a jumbo jet to New York. Another unknown. I didn't want any of my friends to see me off at the airport. No more goodbyes.

This time I'm flying in style. I enter the aircraft and the steward at the entrance greets me with a smile as he checks my boarding pass.

'Welcome aboard Madame,' he gestures with his hand, 'up the stairs, don't stop 'til you reach the stars.'

I settle back into the luxury of real leather with lots of leg room and no one beside me.

The plane gathers momentum as it races across the tarmac and, with hardly a thud, we're airborne. Strangely, I'm very calm.

I look out of the cabin window. Below I can make out the river and there is the large white monument in Piazza Venezia.

Just before the plane turns its nose to the west, I catch a glimpse of the Colosseum.

I'm sad to be leaving Rome, but I've made some wonderful friends, who I know will remain so, and I'm taking some unforgettable, cherished memories with me:

Greeting my neighbours on the street who know me as the *insegnante inglese:* Walking into the local bar every morning as they are making my *cappuccino bollente*, delivered to me with a *buongiorno* and a flourish: The smell of freshly-baked bread from the bakery: The calls of the market traders, displaying fresh produce from local farmers: And the fountains, always the fountains.

These are some of the things I'll remember and miss about Rome, and of course, Alessandro.

I don't know what's going to happen with Frankie, but I'm prepared to take a chance. I know if it doesn't work out with him in New York, I will return to Rome and to Alessandro, who will still be in Piazza Navona, as promised, *come una lampada*.

But that will be another story.

Epilogue

I stayed in New York for five years and then returned to Rome where, as promised, Alessandro was waiting for me *come una lampada* in Piazza Navona.

    The Euro replaced the Lira.
    Termini had a make-over. The starlings return every year.
    Pasquino Cinema in Trastevere closed for renovation and expansion.
    Cinecitta goes from strength to strength with films such as *The Talented Mr. Ripley* and *The English Patient* to its credit.
    Pope John Paul II died.
    Rome's feral cats are falling in numbers, but the colony still exists in Villa Borghese.
    There are 'gladiators' with plastic swords in the Colosseum.
    The fountains are still flowing.
    Franca still confuses kitchen with chicken.
    Luana and Gianni still enjoy dancing.
    Marco is a handsome teenager. His sister Monica loves me to tell her the story of her baptism.
    Ani and Chris divorced. Ani returned to Canada and married another Chris. They have a baby daughter, Francesca. Chris married another girl with Latino looks. They have a son, Leonardo.
    Dawn lives in Canada where she is happily married.
    Gayle returned to Rome shortly after my departure, for 'closure'.
    Eugene is sunning himself, like a lizard, *come una lucertola*, in his native Bermuda.
    Frankie remains in America. We are still soul mates.

Acknowledgements

This memoir would never have been written without the encouragement and support of my daughter and my friends who, on numerous occasions after I had recounted my experiences to them, told me I should write a book.

My thanks to Marie Rowe for introducing me to Gayle Oliver, without whose encouragement I would probably never have left my native shores to live and work in Rome; for her unwavering support during my first few months in Rome I am eternally grateful. Thanks to both Marie and Gayle for their help with the manuscript and to Nena Bierbaum for her helpful advice and suggestions.

Thanks also to Gerard Sebastian and Marco Caserta for their wonderful illustrations.

Heartfelt thanks to my adopted Italian family who took me into their homes and their hearts as I dove headlong into Italian life: Doctor Francesca Gambera for showing me the Rome that visitors seldom see; Luana and Gianni Balducci for taking me under their wing and for saving my life, and Susanna and Gianni Caserta for welcoming me into their family and entrusting me with their children, Marco and Monica.

Thanks to Eugene de Couto, Christopher Ballard, Anna-Maria Naturalli, Dawn Keneally, Heather Webster and Eleanor Ciafardoni, for their valuable friendship: To my students Stefano Ricci, Petr Parizek and Stefano Fumigalli who made teaching so enjoyable.

Special thanks to Alessandro Scrocca for the romance, and to Francesco 'Frankie' Caero, my special friend and soul mate.